I0048723

ADVANCE PRAISE

"Built on Belief is what happens when a world-class leader finally shares his playbook. When Matt was leading our teams at Apple, he made belief tangible—it shaped how we operated, how we showed up, and how we grew. Now, he's captured that wisdom in a way that's accessible, inspiring, and deeply practical. A must-read for any leader serious about building something meaningful, lasting—and extraordinary."

—STEPHANIE FEHR, CHIEF PEOPLE OFFICER AT UNITEDHEALTHCARE

"Reading Built on Belief felt like sitting in one of Matt's team meetings—where the conversation always starts with purpose, ends in action, and somehow expands your understanding of purposeful leadership. This book captures that rare gift. It's practical, powerful, and full of lived wisdom."

—BRIGITTE KLEINE, CEO OF KHAITE

"Culture doesn't compete with strategy—it's what gives it power. In Built on Belief, Matt Marcotte shows that the most impactful brands are born from intention rooted in meaning. This book challenges leaders to go beyond managing work and start leading with purpose. When people understand why the work matters, they engage more deeply. And when culture reflects that meaning, it drives belonging, fuels performance, and creates the conditions for lasting, meaningful success."

—BRIAN SOLIS, FUTURIST, 9X BESTSELLING AUTHOR OF MINDSHIFT: TRANSFORM LEADERSHIP, DRIVE INNOVATION, AND RESHAPE THE FUTURE

"Built on Belief is that rare leadership book that invites you to pause, reflect, and act with intention. Matt Marcotte's insights are rooted in a deep understanding of both brands and behavior. Drawing from decades of hands-on experience, he offers not quick fixes but proven systems—crafted for leaders who value meaning as much as results. If you're serious about building a culture people truly believe in, this book deserves a permanent spot on your desk."

—ALEX DRINKER, CHIEF CRM OFFICER AT PUBLICIS

"I've seen Matt walk into complex environments and spark lasting transformation—because he understands people, culture, and belief better than anyone. This book captures that rare gift and delivers a field guide for creating cultures that don't just perform—they inspire. This is a must-read for leaders who are serious about building something that lasts."

—DARCY PENICK, FORMER PRESIDENT OF BERGDORF GOODMAN

"In Built on Belief, Matt Marcotte delivers a rare synthesis of cultural intelligence and strategic acuity. Framing cultures of commitment as the ultimate performance driver, he argues that belief—deep, shared, and intentional—is what scales sustainably.

For executives navigating complexity at speed, Built on Belief offers a compelling thesis: Competitive advantage is no longer built on process but on purpose codified in practice. Read this if you are serious about transforming culture from a narrative into an engine."

—ANTHONY ABBATIELLO, CEO ADVISOR, TOP 25 HUMAN CAPITAL CONSULTANTS

"In our relentless pursuit of results, Matt stops us in our tracks, reminding us of the humanity in our work, where magic resides in the sustainable, impactful power of belief. For decades, Matt's commitment to purpose has been a lighthouse for all who pursue growth. Built on Belief is universal, inspiring, and practical, encouraging us to consistently integrate 'Heart, Head, and Hands' to create a brighter future for ourselves and our teams."

—CHRIS PHILLIPS, SVP AND GMM AT JCPENNEY

BUILT ON BELIEF

built on belief

why cultures of
commitment are
the competitive
advantage

matt marcotte

LIONCREST
PUBLISHING

COPYRIGHT © 2025 MATT MARCOTTE
All rights reserved.

BUILT ON BELIEF
Why Cultures of Commitment Are the Competitive Advantage

FIRST EDITION

ISBN 978-1-5445-4989-7 *Hardcover*
      978-1-5445-4988-0 *Paperback*
      978-1-5445-4990-3 *Ebook*
      978-1-5445-4987-3 *Audiobook*

To my Parents:

You believed in me before I had the language for dreams.

*Because of you, I leap. Because of you, I trust
the ground will rise to meet me.*

*Your belief gave me roots and wings. I will never be able to repay
the gift of your love, but I carry it in everything I build.*

To my Husband:

You are my anchor and my horizon.

*You remind me that growth and grounding can coexist, that
the truest partnerships expand us while holding us steady.*

Your unwavering support gave me the freedom to chase my dreams.

You are, simply, the love of my life.

I believe—because you all believed first.

Contents

This book is a testament to the transformative power of belief—and I am its living proof.

When your people believe in what you believe in—and when they know they have your understanding and support—the sky is the limit.

Introduction

When was the last time you really thought about what your brand believes? About your brand's vision and the journey you promise to take people on? How about your external customers? Even more importantly, when was the last time you really thought about the fuel that makes everything happen: your employees? They're the people I refer to as your internal customers. Focusing on them is at the heart of this book.

What do you believe about your people? How do you connect with them? How do you value them? Nurture them? How do you express what you believe and why you exist in ways that create scalable, repeatable, sustainable, and profitable MAGIC because your people believe?

I've had an incredibly blessed career, having worked for some of the most successful, respected, and beloved brands in the world, including Gap, Apple, Tory Burch, Bergdorf, and Salesforce. I've worked alongside hundreds of leaders and thousands of employees, and I've observed and advised countless brands across multiple industries. One thing I've learned is this: too many brands treat their employees and their customers as means to an end, mere vehicles for top-line sales and bottom-line profit.

I believe in something much different: that profit is our reward for doing the right thing. And the right thing involves focusing on and investing in our internal customers. Most companies say they understand the importance of investing in relationships with customers, but they're usually only talking about external customers. Unless you are built and prepared to prioritize your internal customers, you will never be able to translate your brand promise to the people who actually shop with you, purchase from you, and engage with you.

Profit is our reward for doing the right thing. And the right thing involves focusing on and investing in our internal customers.

Here's why: when you invest in internal customers...when you support, challenge, develop, and truly value them...they willingly embody your brand. Their passion radiates throughout every employee and customer interaction that follows as they live, breathe, and share your brand's values with authenticity. They take things you both believe in, make them their own, and convey these beliefs outward. When this happens, you've achieved the essence of a committed culture. And it all begins with belief.

That's what this book is about: tapping into and sustaining belief in your brand in order to build and maintain powerful relationships and drive transformational results at every level.

KNOWING WHAT YOUR BRAND BELIEVES

No company has ever operated their way to greatness. Great leaders are aware that their jobs are to *lead* people while *managing* processes, not the other way around. First, leaders must be clear about what the brand believes. Then they have to rally others so they can buy into this belief. How? Leaders must help them see what's in it for them and recognize how they're a part of the journey. Once belief becomes a shared vision, a brand can build and execute strategies, plans, and goals and achieve incredible results together.

> No company has ever operated their way to greatness. Great leaders lead people and manage processes—not the other way around.

It may seem like many of today's leadership challenges are more complex than ever, but they're fairly universal. After all, humans have similar needs across all experiences. We're tribal. We're wired to connect, and we actively seek these connections at nearly every turn. This is at the heart of all human relationships, which includes the relationships and connections we build with brands.

In the world of brands, customer connections validate that the brand cares about creating authentic, reciprocal, mutually beneficial relationships. The thing is these connections don't happen in a vacuum. They start with a brand's people...with *your* brand's people. They're the ones who drive customer participation, loyalty, and results.

Once belief becomes a shared vision, a brand can build and execute strategies, plans, and goals and achieve incredible results together.

When your people believe in what you believe in, and when they know they have your understanding and support, the sky is the limit.

BELIEF FUELS COMMITMENT

You're going to see the word "commitment" a lot throughout this book. You'll also see the word "compliance," often in comparison. A culture of compliance is one in which employees are good at checking boxes and keeping their heads above water; a culture of commitment is one in which employees believe in and care about your brand at a deep and personal level.

People don't *tread water* in a committed environment. They help steer the ship, especially when they know you see, hear, care for, challenge, reward, and support them. Your actions tell them that you believe in them, which creates a reciprocal exchange. This type of brand expression builds even more commitment, creating a compounding charge as people continue to commit on their own terms in ways that align with your brand's truths and values.

If your brand wants to turn compliance into commitment, it must inspire a level of belief that cycles through employees and reaches out to customers—perhaps even to the world at large. Your brand *needs* your people to strive to build connections with others on emotional levels and to care about creating mutually beneficial relationships that drive increased participation, loyalty, and profitability.

From this perspective, let me add something that might be a little controversial: not every person (employee or customer) will be the right fit for your brand; likewise, your brand won't be the right fit for every person. This is okay.

Here's a bit of a reality check: transforming compliance into genuine commitment is a serious challenge. You can't simply dictate, demand, or wedge commitment into a checklist. That would just be more compliance. It sounds about as exciting as "forced family fun." Sadly, I've seen plenty of brands try to do this very thing. They always fail. We're talking authenticity here. You have to inspire true belief in employees who represent your brand to the outside world. And it's not easy. In fact, it takes more work to achieve commitment than compliance, but it's worth it.

However, when you pull off the switch from compliance to commitment, the belief you instill fuels even more commitment via a deep sense of shared purpose. Your employees aren't just following orders. They're literally moving with you, driven by a shared vision. And when everyone is rowing in the same direction, united in belief, extraordinary things happen.

MORE THAN SOFT SKILLS

My goal with *Built on Belief* is to provide the right dose of stories, tips, and insight to help your brand and you as a leader move past any reluctance and discover how important it is to make belief a cornerstone of your brand's ethos. My career spans over three decades, multiple countries, and three continents. I've worked with global brands when they were growing, at their peak, and after they'd lost their way and were trying to scramble back. I've seen and experienced the vast difference between cultures of compliance and those of commitment.

As much as my career informs these pages, some of my own belief in this work also comes from lessons I've learned in my personal life. I've always been a very outgoing and curious person, and I'm extremely interested in other people: who they are, what they care about, and what they bring to the world. Growing up, part of me was always hiding due to being gay. When I was younger, I realized that fully opening up as my true self wasn't always an option while still trying to be in the world.

As a result, I wound up developing a high level of emotional intelligence in order to navigate various situations. I became really good at *reading the room*, so to say, understanding the machinations of any group I was in and being able to shift energy to create a safer environment.

Here's how this is relevant to the work I've done for the past three decades: I became very in-tune with people, including their motivations, behaviors, and habits. I learned how to put this knowledge to use in order to connect with others, build relationships, and influence outcomes. In other words, how to lead.

At the time I didn't think of anything I was doing as training for my future career with global brands. I was simply figuring out how to be *me* in a world that wasn't always friendly to who I was. Once I entered the corporate world in my early twenties, I started to see the link between my natural tendencies toward connection and curiosity, and my success in business.

For the most part, my focus in business has always been about human capital. I care deeply about people: understanding them, motivating them, developing them, and trying to give as many people as possible a voice in any given situation. The more I was around people, the more curious I grew about understanding our shared environments. My natural curiosity turned into strategic inquiry as I started to build company cultures and focus on employee and customer experiences. I would ask things like "What are we solving for at the highest level?" "Where are we starting from?" "What do we need to do for people to really commit to this?" Years later, these types of questions still form my starting mantra when I'm working to build understanding at the deepest level before moving forward.

BELIEF STARTS IN THE HEART

A framework I have used for years has strangely created disagreement among some friends, colleagues, and professional peers, even as intuitive as it is to me (or at least seems to be). It begins with the idea of starting with the heart, then moving to the head, and finally to the hands. Similar to how a great story works, we first *feel* our way into something. Then we intellectualize it, tossing it around to uncover what it means for us. Finally, after all of the feeling and thinking, we move into action and begin doing.

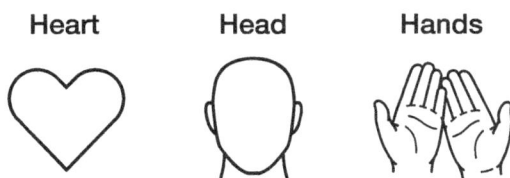

Heart	Head	Hands

Here's the disconnect: if you search these same words online ("Heart, Head, Hands," in that order), the results you'll get back will reorder the words so "head" comes first, then "heart," and finally "hands." That order, with "head" leading the way, is a more widely accepted framework. Personally, I think the algorithms are wrong on this.

Based on everything I have learned, this is not how humans

experience the world of belief. We're emotional beings. The way we *feel* about something alerts us, opens up our ability to hear, internalize, and understand, which drives our willingness to take action.

Everything I'll focus on in the book starts with the heart, where we feel things like *belief* and *connection*. From there, it cycles upward to the head, where we scrutinize, assess, and strategize a way forward. Then we move outward into our hands and actions, and express the things we believe in every day with the hope of creating a contagion of connection with others.

This methodology is absolutely the same for employees as it is for customers. The tactics may look different, but the core is unchanged. For the sake of conversation and because I believe in a classic tagline from an early 2000s ad campaign, "Happy cows make happy cheese," I'm going to focus on your employees throughout the book. They're the drivers of every potential customer relationship.

The alignment between the Heart, Head, and Hands—how we feel, what we think, and what we do—is critical to success. If our notion of belief, or a brand's notion of belief, is nothing more than an exercise in wordsmithing focused on the head and hands, then that's where it will live and die. Think about how many times you have passed brand vision and values on a poster in the breakroom without any measurable or meaningful attributing actions.

The alignment between the Heart, Head and Hands—how we feel, what we think, and what we do—is critical to success.

You must possess belief to make your brand work. And your strategy must be rooted in this belief. That's the basis of how everything comes together. If you want employees to create incredible brand experiences for customers, you have to be inspirational. You also have to create a plan to help them move forward.

A FRAMEWORK FOR RELATIONSHIPS

Heart, Head, Hands is a framework I live by. There's another framework I've created and used in my years building and leading brands that comes from this idea: relationships are critical to brand success no matter how a brand measures this success. Relationships follow their own trajectory. They don't just happen on their own, and you can't force them.

This framework is one I'll share with you in part two of this book. It's a simplification of a natural human relationship journey that covers five core intangibles that exist at the heart of any relationship: Connecting, Assessing, Delivering, Exceeding, and Transforming. You can use this framework at scale to create alignment, improve understanding, build strategy, and ultimately achieve repeatable, scalable, profitable results.

Here's a very simple visual to give you a sense of the framework's cyclical nature:

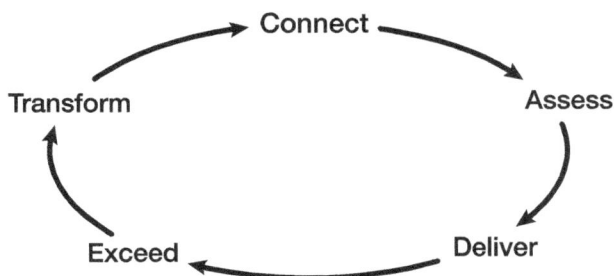

Now for something interesting I discovered about myself while I was writing this book: the idea of putting this framework into the world as a stand-alone concept was bothering me.

First, there is no shortage of frameworks in the world of leadership and brand strategy. And to make matters worse, as an acronym it spells out the word CADET. Brands *love* creating different selling models that spell out words. I wish mine didn't, but it does.

So if this framework could be written off as just another acronym, why did I feel that it was so different from the ones that I had learned early in my career? Well, for one, the CADET framework isn't just different from others, but it also works.

It works for two reasons. The first is that it isn't about artificial steps or prescriptive actions. It is a simplified journey of human relationship building that allows for freedom within the framework. The other, and vastly more important, reason is that the reason this approach has worked for the brands that I led is that the people who used it also helped to create it and fully believed in the power of it. Without that commitment to the vision, this could have become another in a long line of well-meaning "programs" that never went anywhere. That is the real secret sauce—being surrounded by people at all levels and in all roles across your brand who believe and are bound together by clear direction and focus yet given the ability to add themselves to the process.

So, I'm not here to sell you a framework. I'm here to offer a tool and a way to focus on what really matters: building authentic relationships and anchoring belief at the center of everything your brand does. When you understand the power of belief, when you embody it, you can communicate it in ways that inspire employees and win the trust of leaders whose buy-in you need. The framework is just that...a framework. It's not the point; it's the path.

SHARING YOUR VISION TO SPARK BELIEF IN OTHERS

Humans make lots of decisions based on emotion. We ask questions like "Does this *seem* right? What's my *gut* saying? How do I *feel* about this?" Starting from such emotional spaces, we switch over to facts and data, which either pull us deeper into what we feel or push us away. This is part of why storytelling or great speeches can be so incredibly powerful: they're all about emotional resonance. To paraphrase Simon Sinek: "MLK said, 'I have a dream,' not 'I have a plan.'" You don't hinge beliefs on plans. You create plans in order to make beliefs and dreams become reality.

From this perspective, one of the first steps involved in creating a culture of belief is to help others feel their way into the process. You share your vision, then you bring them into the fold in ways that put them in the driver's seat. And the reason is simple: it isn't just about *your* belief; it has to be about *theirs*.

> You don't hinge beliefs on plans. You create plans in order to make beliefs and dreams become reality.

Parlaying this idea into scalable, repeatable, sustainable, and profitable results happens when other people believe in what you believe. They have to want to go the extra mile, push for better outcomes, and deliver excellence because it's personal to them. I'll come back to this theme throughout the book.

Is there a simple equation to any of this? Not exactly. For the sake of trying, this book breaks things down in ten chapters across three parts:

- Part 1 is all about your brand. Do you know what your brand believes? Does *it* know? Has the brand codified its beliefs? We'll begin exploring your brand's beliefs in Chapter 1, and we'll return to the idea of codification at different times throughout the book. We'll also take a look at nurturing employees who believe the same things and building an organizational culture that coalesces around what you believe, and that enables this belief to survive.
- Part 2 will focus on the first three phases of the CADET framework: **connecting**, **assessing**, and **delivering**. In my view, these are table stakes for any brand that cares about its people and its customers.
- Part 3 is where we'll lift off as we aspire toward **exceeding** and ultimately **transforming**. From there, we'll wrap up with a conversation about your north star, which serves as a reminder that this work never ends.

My hope is that this book reinforces your own concept of belief and commitment, or at least opens your eyes to the idea. It's not a how-to book or a "do this/don't do that" manual. There's nothing prescriptive in these pages. Instead, I've chosen to lean into some stories from my career as a way to flash light on a few different paths.

In the end, nothing extraordinary and transformational happens without commitment. To arrive there, you start with belief. It's the underpinning of everything that follows. That's where we'll begin Chapter 1. First, a question: what does your brand believe?

> **In the end, nothing extraordinary and transformational happens without commitment.**

Part 1

Brands have to be crystal clear about what they stand for, what their offerings are, what their core promise is, what space they want to hold in the world, and how that space makes them unique.

CHAPTER 1

What Does Your Brand Believe?

Belief starts with emotion (heart), moves through strategy (head), and translates into action (hands). But this isn't just about believing. It's about turning belief into smart, strategic actions that create a lasting impact on employees, customers, and the world.

Brands cast interesting spells. They can shape a person's individuality and bring us into a community at the same time. The right sneaker, smart phone, handbag, car, whatever it is, helps to tell the world who we are and how we see ourselves. The logo reinforces a sense of identity and belonging, whether it's a swoosh on a T-shirt or the outline of a once-bitten apple on the back of a smartphone.

Brands are especially powerful when rooted in emotional connection. This is where I thrive. I've lived this truth for more than thirty years as a leader inside some of the world's most recognizable brands. Throughout my career, I've never been a hired gun but a steward of each brand I've been a part of. I've believed in its vision, culture, and what it stands for. What has fueled my success has been my ability to turn belief into a strategic advantage—a worldview that can be codified and implemented across organizations and oceans.

Brands are especially powerful when rooted in emotional connection.

Even today before I even consider joining a company or partnering with a brand, I ask and answer questions like these:

- Is the brand clear on what it is, why it exists, and what it is solving for?
- Do I believe in this brand's mission and what they're doing in the world?
- Do I align with their culture and values?
- Are they willing to invest in building a strategy that expresses their vision fully and confidently even when times get tough?
- Will I have the support I need in order to express the brand's DNA in a way that gets others invested in their success?
- Do I have responsibility AND authority?

These aren't just checklist questions. They're clarity questions. They help me determine whether I can do what I do best: not just express a brand but amplify it at scale.

EMOTIONAL ATTACHMENTS TO BRANDS

There are thousands of brands out there. There are also thousands of companies that *think* they are brands but aren't. Real brands communicate authenticity and a specific point of view. That means that, by design, brands are not for everyone. And that's okay. As soon as you try to be everything for everyone, the core of who and what your brand is begins to unravel.

I saw this happen firsthand when I was at Gap. At the time, the brand was one of the darlings of Wall Street. They were growing, and then they weren't. And the attempt to restart growth was actually one of the things that caused them to slip away from their existing ethos and lose sight of their core customer in the process.

Going after the tween market was a "calculated" risk—a decision made in the *head* (read: management consultants) without giving thought to the *heart* of the brand. The result: our core customers felt alienated and forgotten, and soon they took their business elsewhere. Meanwhile, the tween customer had no emotional connection to the brand. They cherry picked the product, mostly at a discount.

I'm going to share some other stories from my time at Gap throughout this book. I'm bringing this up now to illustrate an important point: brands have to be crystal clear about what they stand for, what their offerings are, what their core promise is, what space they want to hold in the world, and how their space makes them unique. The sharper that clarity, the easier it becomes to make bold decisions, evolve the business, and pursue new opportunities without ever losing sight of the brand's core DNA.

When a brand operates from that level of clarity, it can confidently move forward, bringing loyal customers along for the journey while attracting new ones who align with its beliefs. That's how you grow without losing who you are.

Great brands understand that they don't just sell products. They stand for something. They exist for people who see themselves reflected in the brand's values, who want to be part of something larger than themselves. But to attract those people, a brand must first be unmistakably clear about its own beliefs.

> **Great brands understand that they don't just sell products. They stand for something.**

By and large, the relationships we have with brands are emotional in nature. Why else would we buy a $5,000 vinyl bag for the logo or opt for the $80,000 car when the $30,000 model will get us to and from the grocery store just fine? Something along the way causes us to *believe* in an inherent value certain brands possess. Essentially, we believe in the dream they promise.

There is a saying that vision without execution is just a dream. I believe this saying is absolutely true. But vision isn't where we start. First we attach ourselves to the things *we* believe in. Then we figure out what this belief means and how to make it happen so it goes from dream to reality. Belief fuels vision. Without belief, vision is hollow. Without vision, belief is static.

Here's another saying I like to live by: no one operates themselves to greatness, which I mentioned in the introduction. First, we dream (feel); then we strategize (think); then we build (act). In other words: Heart, Head, Hands. Brands must follow this same course of action.

> **Belief fuels vision. Without belief, vision is hollow. Without vision, belief is static.**

That's not to say that operations don't matter, because they do. Brands become healthier thanks to operational excellence. They're more prepared to scale when their systems are dialed in. Operations are also about cleaning and shoring things up to become super-efficient.

Through the lens of operations, brands look at costs, consider investments, and make sure margins are strong. This is how they "control their controllables," so to say. But operations do not drive top-line results, encourage customers to participate, or get employees excited about showing up to work. That's where belief reigns.

Sadly, when things get difficult, many brands retreat and turn operations into the star of the show. They start scrutinizing every expense and cost point they can cut. Unfortunately, there's only so much a brand can do from an operational standpoint. After all, you can't squeeze blood from a stone. Unless a brand in this situation can drive more sales and also overcome bottom-line headwinds, it cannot grow, which is why operations will only get you so far.

When it comes to growth, every brand must master two things: acquiring new customers and deepening relationships with the ones they already have. Both are essential. But how do brands truly achieve this? It comes down to one thing: *belief*. And the stewards of that belief? Your employees.

Employees are the ones who spot opportunities, build strategies, foster communities, and bring the brand's beliefs to life at every touchpoint. But here's the catch: they can only do this if they have a crystal-clear understanding of *what* the brand believes and are genuinely *committed* to it. That's where leadership comes in. Leaders must create clarity and inspire commitment, turning belief from a concept into a lived experience.

Too often, though, brands jump straight to strategy. They focus on *what* to do before ever addressing *why* anyone should care. They operate in a Head, Heart, Hands sequence, starting with logic, hoping emotion and action will follow. And while that approach might get short-term compliance, it doesn't build the kind of commitment where employees truly believe in the mission and express it authentically to customers.

> **Leaders must create clarity and inspire commitment, turning belief from a concept to a lived experience.**

Real brand growth happens when you flip that model and start with the heart. When belief comes first, strategy becomes more than a plan. It becomes a shared mission. And that's when employees don't just follow the strategy. They truly *own* it.

BUILDING AND MAINTAINING BRAND CULTURE

Lots of brands start off with a culture that expresses their beliefs so profoundly and directly that the brand and its culture become legendary. Sadly, many of these same brands lose their focus and forget what makes them special. It's not intentional or immediate, but rather a slow erosion. They simply forget about their "secret sauce."

At one of the brands I led, I met many amazing people who had a profound love for a brand they remembered: one that focused on exceeding customer expectations and promoted a sense of pride of working at the best place on earth. However, the brand no longer reflected what it had been, and the product, while still amazingly curated and special, wasn't enough to keep the brand relevant.

We needed to reignite the brand's old passion and unleash our people so they could do the one thing they wanted to do: delight customers. We had to remember WHO we were as a brand. We had to go backward so we could go forward. To do so, we focused on the culture.

Our goal: to revisit, refine, and reignite everything about our culture, starting with our employees. We wanted them to guide us...to show us what made us different, special, extraordinary.

Culture needed to be the foundation of any strategy we'd create if we were actually going to get away from merely being *transactional* and get back to being *transformational*. Everyone involved had to believe. From the brand's president on down to the part-time stockroom associate, we all needed to be part of the journey.

During this work, we became very clear about one thing: if you didn't believe or didn't care about reigniting the belief, then perhaps this wasn't the right place. That might read like a hard truth, but here's an even harder one: you cannot turn a ship around if only half the crew is rowing in the same direction.

Recalling this experience points to a key message I want you to keep in mind: no brand can get away with simply checking boxes if its goal is to create meaningful and lasting connections. Here's what that means for you: if your goal is to create a culture of belief, you have to help people feel their way into and through the process.

No brand can get away with simply checking boxes if its goal is to create meaningful and lasting connections.

Before you can do this, your brand needs to address the following three key pieces:

1. KNOW WHAT YOU BELIEVE AND ACCEPT WHAT YOU DON'T BELIEVE.

A brand should not try to be everything to everyone. As you explore what you believe, you have to narrow down to your core belief (or set of beliefs) before you scale up.

2. UNDERSTAND WHAT YOUR EMPLOYEES BELIEVE AND WANT.

What does belief look like to them? What's in it for them? What's missing from their current experience? Are they aligned with the brand beliefs, and if not, how will you handle that?

3. INTRODUCE AND REINFORCE THE IDEA OF ROWING TOGETHER TOWARD A SHARED VISION.

This starts by helping employees understand the brand's *rules of engagement*: the values, behaviors, and expectations that guide how they show up and contribute. When employees know how to bring their best ideas forward and how those ideas connect to the brand's broader mission, they do more than execute. They engage. This alignment creates a clear line of sight between internal belief and external action.

Returning to that earlier story: once we addressed these foundational questions, we were ready to build strategies, processes, and metrics that reinforced what we *believed* while giving employees the autonomy and responsibility to bring that belief to life every day.

This is true for any brand. Your beliefs should be embedded in your culture, not just as words on a wall but as the *operating system* that guides how you see, hear, challenge, engage, uplift, and reward both employees and customers. Belief isn't something you bolt on. It's baked in. It shapes everyone and everything.

BELIEF WILL BUOY YOU WHEN THINGS CHANGE

Let me repeat the question I asked at the end of the introduction: What does your brand believe? Are you conveying these beliefs clearly? Are you living these beliefs in your actions?

The world used to be a much different place for brands. Today it's more crowded than ever with products and services. Plus, barriers to entry are as low as they've ever been, thanks in part to social media, influencer marketing, AI, and a steady rush of new direct-to-consumer products. For a brand to compete, it has to capture customers through engagements, not just from products.

> Belief isn't something you bolt on. It's baked in. It shapes everything and everyone.

Your product is not your brand. It's the souvenir of a much larger and integrated brand experience...a token that fulfills the desire to participate again and again.

From a brand perspective, there are many questions you can

answer on your way toward uncovering and communicating your beliefs. Here are just a few:

- Why do you exist? Clarifying this is an absolute must.
- What is your purpose?
- How are you unique? Knowing this will help you understand your brand's emotional motivators that create links and connections.
- How do you imbue your emotional motivators into your actions? I'm talking about how you support your people and bring them into your beliefs.
- How do you empower employees to embody these actions in their interactions with customers? This is about the way they interact with customers.

> **Your product is not your brand. It's the souvenir of a much larger and integrated brand experience.**

In the end, belief is the cornerstone to everything that follows. Without it, your brand can't create true commitment, which is what every leader wants.

CODIFYING BELIEFS

Brand founders and leaders aren't always comfortable with the topic of codifying their beliefs. Many founders see it being "too corporate" to try to clarify and codify a belief that already seems clear and feels personal to them. The assumption is that people "should just get it." There's a pretty obvious argument against this type of resistance: just because something is clear to one person doesn't mean anyone else in the world will get it or even care about it.

There's also the fact that the process of codifying a belief can be messy and emotional. It can even seem like a "soft skills exercise" in the eyes of some leaders, especially if they're not driving the results or the metrics around how people will measure it.

No matter the case, leaders can find plenty of reasons to just stick with building objectives-based, data-driven strategies and leaning into the idea of creating a culture of compliance that follows directions coming down from the top.

Here's the issue with not codifying what you believe: if the meaning behind who you are and how you show up is nebulous or too open to interpretation, you're giving people license to define your vision in whatever way suits them. Instead of seeing things through your brand's lens of awareness, they'll apply their own.

At first glance, this might sound kind of empowering, but it can be chaotic. Imagine you're driving around somewhere, and it happens to be the day when everyone wants to interpret the meaning of red and green traffic lights. I hope you have your auto body shop and your chiropractor in your contact list.

True, codifying beliefs can be tricky, but it's an extremely important exercise. That's especially true when your brand is scaling, since scaling a culture is difficult for any brand.

I'm going to come back to the topic of codifying beliefs throughout the book. For now, rather than walk you through all of the work involved in codifying beliefs, I want to offer one very important piece of advice: get your employees involved.

Give them agency, a voice, and an opportunity to help create the future. When someone knows their ideas are part of the mix, then they are more willing to put skin in the game. And when that's the case, they are more likely to look for ways to make the vision succeed.

We can all agree that brands are emotional, experiential invitations for relationships. Simon Sinek puts it this way: "People don't buy what you do; they buy why you do it. And what you do simply proves what you believe." In order to express what you believe in a way that resonates authentically, you have to root all of your strategies, plans, and especially actions into it.

As I wrote earlier, belief doesn't do anything on its own. Your people are the ones who do the doing. I'm going to lean into this idea in Chapter 2 and focus on your people.

Curiosity is something many leaders in organizations lack, yet it's the lifeblood of knowledge. It's a mindset that prioritizes asking over assuming, listening over telling, and learning over knowing.

CHAPTER 2

Your People Are Your Secret Sauce

To build organizations of commitment rather than compliance and environments where amazing people are allowed—no, expected—to bring their best, leaders must invite them to participate in creating the future. To do so, employees must have a voice in building the way the brand connects with customers.

My organizations have tended to be among the largest population of employees, with teams across functions and departments, both corporate and in the field, some closer to the end customer, others spread across the country and the world. When you employ thousands or tens of thousands of employees, people with unique roles, perspectives, and personalities, getting them to row in the same direction is critical...and also very hard.

Many companies take what they assume to be the easy way out and focus on compliance, complete with checklists, policies, procedures, and a classic carrot-and-stick, top-down management style.

My approach is different. I aim to harness the profound power of belief. My goal is to inspire and empower people to create transformational experiences, not out of obligation or fear of consequences but from a deep, genuine commitment to a shared vision.

HOW DO YOU BUILD COMMITMENT?

First you have to figure out where you want to go. From there, you have to be very honest about where you are starting from.

The questions that follow, many of which I have asked myself throughout the years leading teams and brands, are just a few examples of the many you could ask. Their secret power is that they focus on understanding people's motivations and are in service to what people find important—not what you find important. For starters:

- Do people understand what we are solving for? Do they agree?
- If not, then what will it take to build alignment?
- Do employees see how their work connects and contributes to the vision of the brand?
- How do you get members of decentralized teams, some of which are scattered across the globe, to feel connected to what the brand believes?
- How can you get people to want to move in the same direction as you?
- Where are they starting from? What do they need?
- What is getting in the way of commitment?

In my years developing leaders, one of the biggest ideas I try to impart is that great leaders ask great questions. They don't tell. They ask. They seek to understand before being understood. They remain curious. In fact, they thrive on being curious.

Curious leaders seek out diverse perspectives, challenge their own thinking, and explore *why* things are the way they are. That way they can imagine *how* they could be better. It's the engine behind growth, innovation, and authentic connection.

**Great leaders ask great questions.
They don't tell. They ask.**

Asking questions is a sign of putting curiosity to work for you. Curiosity is something many senior leaders in organizations lack, yet it's the lifeblood of knowledge. It's a mindset that prioritizes asking over assuming, listening over telling, and learning over knowing. It's also the intentional pursuit of a deeper understanding about people, problems, and possibilities, with the goal of leading more effectively.

Bottom Line: If you want to build a culture of commitment, start with curiosity. Ask questions. Listen deeply. People need to feel seen, heard, and valued for what they *can contribute* before they'll ever choose to go beyond compliance. Commitment is earned through connection.

YOU NEED PEOPLE TO SCALE BELIEF

When your employees love what you believe and they believe in what you're doing, it's easier for them to see how their actions fit the bigger picture. When they see themselves as a part of the vision, strategy, and execution—Heart, Head, Hands—commitment takes root. They don't come to work just because they need a paycheck. They're with you because they want to be there.

I mentioned earlier that scaling a culture is one of the most difficult things any brand can try to do. There are a few reasons why. The best way to crack into a longer discussion is to start by looking at things from a founder's perspective.

Starting a business is incredibly hard. Sustaining it is even harder. And growing it...well, you get the point. When a person or a group of people start a business, there's usually a core belief system that drives them along. Something compels them to venture into the market, hang their shingle, launch their website, set up their socials, and put the word out. When in doubt, they can tap into the founding belief that got them started, then continue to move ahead. Wash, rinse, repeat.

Eventually, they grow. It's no longer just the founders now. Maybe they have a dozen employees one day. In a year, they double their roster. Then they double it again. Then again. There's a bit of disruption and some new systems to learn, but the process works. And that core founding belief resides at the heart of everything.

It's a pretty picture, but it doesn't last. Eventually, more time goes by. The brand now includes fresh faces and plenty of outside energy. Some of the original cast and crew are still around, but there are layers of management and bureaucracy between them and the most recent hires. And many of the upper leadership layers include people who came from other well-known or established brands. They've brought their experiences and views with them...along with their baggage.

This is the moment where the strong beliefs that have carried them from the start must coalesce with people at all levels. If they're not paying attention to what their people believe...aren't hiring people who share their vision...or aren't guiding newcomers the right way, then they're setting up a situation where erosion can set in.

Once beliefs collide, then the brand's core belief about where to focus, what to solve for, when to invest, and how to build, scale, and sustain becomes diluted. In this type of environment, individuals will begin setting up and running with competing agendas. The soul of the brand starts to weaken. Hitting financial metrics will become the new north star.

Don't think this can't happen or doesn't happen. It does all the time. I have seen it happen many times across many brands during my time in industry.

Conversely, plenty of brands scale their cultures incredibly well. One of the best examples I've been a part of was during my time at Apple. When I moved from Gap to Apple, they were already one of the most culturally driven companies in the world. People literally loved them. They still do. But the Apple brand we know today was not always Apple. Back in the early '80s and '90s, the brand was fairly niche, relatively speaking. They had an attitude, but they didn't have market share, at least nowhere near what they have now. Then things began to shift.

In 2001, Apple launched the iPod. In 2002 came the iPod for Windows. That's when things truly exploded.

Let me pause for a moment here. Earlier I wrote that your product is not your brand, yet here I am writing about products. That's because Apple is a prime example of what happens when products are completely aligned with a brand's ethos. Apple's next-gen products literally became the physical manifestation of everything Steve Jobs and the leadership at Apple believed in.

Apple's defining attitude and its core cultural attributes have always been based on pushing against the status quo. Remember their "Think different" campaign? It came complete with the grammatically incorrect "different" (rather than "differently," as the occasional word nerd liked to point out). They didn't care. What they cared about was unleashing creativity. They didn't create the personal computer, MP3 players, or the smartphone. They just made them different...better...more *Apple*.

Okay, back to the story now. As the iPod took off, some of Apple's legacy employees weren't excited about it, or should I say, how it was happening. Apple was *their* thing, not for PC customers. They were the Mac faithful and saw themselves as gatekeepers of the brand. Some were among the earliest employees of Apple stores and weren't too excited about selling iPods to people who didn't even own a Mac.

This attitude wasn't a recipe for scaling, which we knew. We had to figure out how to deal with it. We had an incredible opportunity for growth while bringing the goodness of Apple to many more people around the country and the world. What could we do?

We made a decision to try to help these employees see the benefits of PC customers coming into the brand. We made it clear that if they couldn't get on board, then we would help them find a better home somewhere else. It sounds simple on paper, but it was painful, especially considering these employees were the soul of the brand. They'd believed in Apple from the beginning, even during lean years. We knew this could fundamentally change the brand's culture, especially if we handled it wrong. So we focused on doing what was right for the employees, making sure to support them even if this was no longer the right career path.

I started at Apple in the beginning of explosive growth. At the time, we had ten thousand employees, and the brand was on fire. We were opening about fifty stores a year globally. In North America alone, we scaled up to twenty-five thousand employees in just three years. Not only did we have to offboard some of our core culture carriers, but we also had to hire more than twice as many store employees. This could have been a recipe for disaster, and the culture might have changed dramatically and permanently.

As we grew, we remained clear on the core of what Apple was and is: a revolutionary company driven by creativity and disruptive innovation. Our beliefs, values, approaches, and culture, all of which were codified, were not going to change. And we were committed to doubling down on them, making sure our employees understood the brand's origin and its vision for the future.

As part of the hiring process, we needed to be clear about the attributes we were looking for. Did we want more hardcore technologists? People who could fix computers? People who could teach others how to use Macs and the growing list of products and applications?

While hiring toward these attributes would have been wonderful, there just weren't enough candidates to fill all the openings we had and expected to have in the next few years. Instead, we focused on hiring people who loved being in service to customers, shared Apple's values, and wanted people to love the brand as much as they did. We knew we could teach new hires the technical things and focused on hiring for the heart, then building a culture of belief.

BELIEF GOES BOTH WAYS

I mentioned earlier how important it is to be very intentional when it comes to your brand's cultural beliefs. The early steps in creating any culture begin by defining what you want the culture to be, then codifying this definition. Even this process runs the risk of becoming nothing more than spewing words on paper if you lose sight of your people and what they believe in.

If belief doesn't flow in both directions, then it's not flowing at all. You need reciprocity. Belief isn't a straight line or an arrow stuck in a tree. It's a loop that cycles through itself. In any belief-based culture of commitment, the brand must show their people that it believes in them.

The people we hired at Apple believed in the things Apple believed in. And they understood that Apple believed in them. How? Let me go back to our hiring and the emphasis we placed on customer care and brand passion.

If belief doesn't flow in both directions, then it's not flowing at all. You need reciprocity.

No matter how much our people loved the brand, we couldn't overlook the fact that our customers were getting savvier by the day. They didn't want to come to our stores with questions only to leave without answers. Our people needed to be ready to give customers what they wanted.

To hit this reality straight on, Apple made the decision to hire and populate new stores at least two weeks ahead of opening. Our employees spent those two weeks training, learning, and completing tutorials, effectively getting paid to become experts before the new store earned a dime. This was not the norm in our industry at the time. It was its own kind of revolutionary decision. In short, it was a *very Apple* thing to do.

Even better, while people were getting this cultural education into all-things Apple, the new stores were experiencing a great deal of group synergy as various pieces of a strong team came together. By the time the stores opened, it was like they'd been operating for a year. As a brand, we were doing our best to align expectations with resources; we were asking people to do the same. And we were making sure they had everything they needed to be successful.

This drive didn't stop once the stores opened. We also knew that our employees had lives outside of work. There were plenty of cases in which part of why we hired certain people came down to how excited they were about their own life experiences and the part Apple products played in them. All throughout our stores, you'd find artists, writers, musicians, actors, freelance designers, indie filmmakers...people who loved our brand because of what the brand did for them on a daily basis.

Many of these employees were still very active in their creative projects and wanted to be able to pursue their passions outside of work as well as inside the brand. So we tried to structure things in such a way that made it easier to encourage and support our employees' endeavors.

Whenever possible, we wanted them to pursue their creative goals without worrying about losing their jobs. To us, it was important for them to know they could work here, but they could also take off with their band for a week or travel to a film shoot or disappear for a few days to work on their screenplay. We wanted them to know they were important to us because of who they were and what they loved, not a means to an end or a tool to help us make a sale.

OPTIMISM CREATES INSPIRATION

A culture of belief is a culture of optimism and inspiration. When a group of people believe in what you're doing and they know you believe in them, their minds focus on the potential in front of them. They start to wonder, "What's possible? What can we do *better*? How great can we be together?"

A pervasive energy comes from working toward what's possible. It's the type of energy every brand wants and no brand ever wants to lose. It's an energy where the focus is on building and being a part of something that is going to be bigger than people can imagine.

A culture of belief is a culture of optimism and inspiration.

When people rally around belief, they understand that the most important first step is holding onto this belief, then exploring what you have to do in order to make something happen. Obviously there are going to be hard or tricky times. Change will find its way to you, and it won't always be positive. If belief is there at the beginning and you and other leaders are reinforcing it, then you encourage your people to stay focused on possibilities.

One of the most important jobs of any leader is to be inspirational. You want to motivate people to bring their best and inspire them into action. Your authenticity, energy, and passion conspire to create inspiration. With this in mind, let me ask you point-blank: if you don't believe in something, how can you expect to get other people to believe in it? Speaking personally, I know for a fact that I've never inspired anyone to do anything that I myself did not believe in.

What happens when you have someone or a group of people who don't believe or who stop believing? Well, for one, they may need help finding a new place where they feel more aligned. That's okay. People move around all the time. But what about those people who get stuck on obstacles? Is this the same thing as not believing?

CULTURE, CULTURE, CULTURE

Belief isn't static. It's dynamic, like an actual relationship. It oscillates and changes all day, every day. Since we're emotional beings, we can all be temperamental at times. We fall in and out of love with people, and we do the same with brands.

How does a brand keep the love alive with its people? The most essential way is through ongoing investment—but not in the way you might think. This isn't just about salaries or perks. Yes, compensation matters, but it's rarely the only reason people choose to leave. Time and again, research shows that culture and leadership are the real drivers of retention. They can also drive turnover for that matter. You can find many reports out there that refer to "toxic cultures" as being the main reason why employees walk away.

People join companies but leave leaders, and the way you treat your people determines whether they stay committed, especially in times of change.

When leaders meet employees with respect, dignity, and genuine care, that trust builds resilience, carrying the team through uncertainty. But when leaders reduce people to being the means to an end and only value them for what they produce, the connection erodes.

Commitment isn't something you can demand. You earn it through your daily actions and the relationships you build on mutual respect. Likewise, you can't expect resilience to suddenly emerge during hard times. You have to cultivate it long before difficult times arrive.

RECOMMITTING AS YOU SCALE

When I shared the Apple story I shared earlier, I was focused on the fact that your people are key when it comes to scaling your culture. What happens to your brand's core beliefs as it scales from a hundred to a thousand employees, from a thousand to five thousand, and on and on? And what can you do to ensure the brand's truths cycle into your employees' actions?

Commitment isn't something you can demand. You earn it through your daily actions and the relationships you build on mutual respect.

What I've learned is that when things stretch out and growth happens, the feelings and meanings that define a brand can get watered down, forgotten, or even lost. As a leader in this situation, I believe it's helpful to pull people together periodically in order to recenter and reaffirm that you are all still operating from the same system of beliefs.

Whether offsite or onsite, these types of gatherings can help you reengage and reinspire people. It doesn't matter if you're leading conversations or you're using these moments as a platform for listening and connecting; it's another way to illustrate that belief is a loop. These check-ins can create their own type of transformational outcomes.

Over the years, I've planned hundreds of offsites for teams, and I've relied on a few essential filters to guide every decision. Here are four I've found incredibly powerful:

- Pass every decision about what you discuss through the Heart, Head, Hands filter: "How do I want people to feel when they leave?" "What do I want them to think when they leave?" "What do I want them to do when they leave?"
- Use the time together in person for things you can only do

in person. Don't put topics on the agenda that could be an email or a conference call.

- Have a connective thread throughout the time together. A narrative arc helps to create emotional connection and understanding and also helps to edit what you don't talk about as much as what you do talk about.
- Use every minute to create and reinforce connection to each other and the brand.

Employees work for a company two-hundred sixty days a year. If you are lucky, you get to bring them together on four of those days. Be clear on what you are solving for. Do the work. Invest the energy. Make it matter.

You and I both know that every brand hits inflection points. New leadership steps in, markets shift, downturns happen, and customers drift away. The natural response should be to pause, reset, and reevaluate through the lens of the brand's core beliefs. Yet, too often, brands skip this work entirely.

Momentum doesn't sustain itself. It needs attention. One image that comes to mind for me is a spinning top. With the right start, it moves with energy, speed, and balance. It looks effortless, perhaps even self-sustaining. But eventually, without continued input, it begins to wobble. The spin slows. The focus falters. And finally, it tips over.

Cultures are no different.

You can launch with clarity. Inspire belief. Spark real motion. But if you stop paying attention, or you assume momentum will carry itself, the energy will fade. Alignment drifts. The commitment cracks. That's why belief isn't a one-time message. It's a *practice*.

Momentum doesn't sustain itself. It needs attention.

The most enduring leaders are the ones who keep giving that top a gentle push. A nudge of clarity. A reminder of purpose. A moment of connection. Momentum may start with a spark, but you have to sustain it with care.

These inflection points aren't just about crises. They show up in growth too. What gets you from $100 million to $200 million is one thing; getting from $200 million to $500 million is an entirely different game that requires other tools, mindsets, and expectations.

Here's the truth: no matter how you're trying to scale, the moment you start neglecting your people, you're already struggling upstream with weights tied to your ankles. If employees don't believe you care about them, why should they care about the brand? That's when people disengage, default to checklists, and settle into compliance. And that's why so many brands stall or sink.

The moment you start neglecting your people, you're already struggling upstream with weights tied to your ankles.

On that note, let's explore those waters in Chapter 3. We need to identify the smell they're giving off.

In the end, being anchored in a culture of compliance prevents people, teams, work groups, and brands from actually reaching new horizons.

CHAPTER 3

Smells Like Compliance to Me

How would you define the culture of your workplace: one of compliance or of commitment? Here's a general rule: compliance needs supervision; commitment builds partnerships.

Compliance and commitment deliver vastly different results. Throughout this chapter I'm going to compare the two. This will help you get a sense of the culture you're currently in, as well as the type of culture you want to create. Are you in a place that inspires commitment? Or is your brand more interested in steering people toward compliance?

THE COMPLIANCE TRAP

Why do companies choose a culture of compliance rather than one of commitment? For starters, compliance is a seemingly easier road to take. All it requires is that people follow rules they did not help to create.

Focusing on checking boxes is a sign of compliance. There is nothing strategic about compliance. It is a game of tactical execution. Giving employees a checklist to mark off is basically the same as handing them the answers to a test. They'll give you the exact experience and answers you're looking for; they might even do so happily, without having to worry about thinking for themselves.

In the end, being anchored in a culture of compliance prevents people, teams, work groups, and brands from actually reaching new horizons. While many organizations that run on compliance stay afloat, they don't go as far as they could.

I'll go so far as to say that an environment that follows a compliance mindset is happy being mediocre. In this environment, you don't need innovators. You just need people to execute on what's in front of them. To that point, compliance literally dictates things like getting in line, following orders, and implementing strategies someone else created. Input isn't necessary, just output. In these types of cultures, the best talent leaves and underperformers stay.

Companies with compliance-driven cultures often *talk* about values and beliefs, but the real test is whether those ideals align with how the culture actually operates. If a company's beliefs genuinely match its compliance-first approach, there's at least transparency. Employees know exactly what's expected, and they can decide whether that environment is right for them. The real trouble begins when there's a disconnect between what a brand *claims* to value and how it *actually* treats its people. That's when trust erodes and the culture begins to break down.

Let's be clear: compliance can look polished on the surface. It appeals to operators because it promises consistency and control. Some leaders will even argue that compliance ensures standards across a brand. And yes, it can, but only through enforcement, not engagement. It's a system built on consequences, powered by the familiar carrot-and-stick approach.

In compliance cultures, behaviors often follow a predictable pattern:

- Employees show up on time not out of pride but out of fear of being written up.
- They greet customers on cue because the script tells them to, not because they genuinely want to connect.
- They keep the store clean because a corporate visit or secret shopper might show up unannounced.
- They check all the boxes because they've learned exactly which hoops to jump through to stay in good standing.

The truth is a culture of compliance ultimately works *against* the brand.

- It stifles the very qualities that drive exceptional performance because it never calls people to bring their best.
- It discourages initiative, ownership, and creative problem-solving, especially when it comes to enhancing the customer experience or strengthening the brand's reputation.
- In these environments, employees rarely feel their voices matter in shaping decisions, strategies, or plans, which leaves little room for true growth or advancement.

COMPLIANCE FOSTERS *JOBS*, NOT CAREERS

It's not forward-thinking; it's box-checking. In compliant cultures, every obstacle becomes a full stop, not a challenge to overcome. Worse, it breeds sameness. People conform because they've learned the unspoken rules: stay in line, don't rock the boat, do just enough to get by.

Which leads to a question: if you haven't inspired your

people to remove obstacles, empowered them to tackle problems in new ways, or equipped them with the tools and support to think boldly, why would you ever expect them to rise above compliance?

> ## In compliant cultures, every obstacle becomes a full stop, not a challenge to overcome.

I just recently ran into a small compliance-minded obstacle when I was trying to treat my father to a holiday dinner in town. I'd made early six o'clock reservations for the two of us at an upscale downtown restaurant. When the date got closer, my father could no longer make it, but I had two friends who had been dying to try the same place. I decided to call a few days before the reservation and see if I could change to a table for three.

I spoke with the host and explained the situation. Then I asked about changing for three. His answer was very quick and certain. "No," he said.

Hmm...I paused for a second and then decided I would try to ask one more time a different way.

"By any chance is there another time that you might be able to fit three of us?" I asked.

"I could get you in at 8:30," he offered almost immediately.

Let's replay this. First, do you see the compliance mindset at play in that scenario? It's subtle, but it's there. How come I, as the customer, had to do extra work to get a table for three?

Based on how quickly he answered my second question, it was clear to me he knew there was availability at 8:30 p.m. What if, instead of "No," his first answer went like this: "I can't fit three of you at 6:00 p.m., but if you're flexible on the time, we have a spot for three at 8:30 p.m. Would that work?"

You may not think these small moments make a difference, but they do. This host in this situation was compliant to the task at hand. I asked, and he answered but offered nothing more. He didn't feel the need to help me eat at his restaurant. He clearly didn't care if I ate at his restaurant. He seemingly didn't care that the revenue attached to the cancellation would be lost, so results weren't a focus for him. He was simply "doing his job" of answering my question.

This is one example of how a compliance mindset plays out in real time. People in such an environment focus on the tasks in front of them, the things they need to knock off before the workday is through. They don't think about moving along the proverbial chess board unless someone else tells them where to move or forces them to move. No one has ever encouraged or allowed them to figure out their own way forward. This leads to lost opportunities, ruins the customer experience, cuts into revenue, and erodes reputations.

Yes...compliance is where brands go to die.

THE PROMISE OF COMMITMENT

Commitment unleashes the best in your people. They're the ones making strategy happen. They're part of the bigger vision and the higher order mission. Their work becomes a vocation for them. Their attachment to outcome pushes them through any barriers. They're committed. They don't just blindly follow someone else's vision. They take part in creating the vision they choose to follow.

Compliance is where brands go to die. Commitment unleashes the best in your people.

Commitment doesn't mean chaos. It's not a free-for-all where anyone does whatever they please. True commitment thrives within a *structure* that comes with clarity and purpose. It's what I call *freedom within a framework*. Rules exist, but they're not arbitrary; they're understood. Employees know why those boundaries are there, how to navigate within them, and where to find the support they need. In this environment, feedback flows naturally, encouraging continuous learning and evolution.

True commitment thrives within a structure that comes with clarity and purpose. It's what I call freedom within a framework.

One of my favorite stories to illustrate this comes from a simple study conducted in 2006 on the relationship between boundaries and creativity. Researchers observed preschoolers at two playgrounds.

One playground had no fence, while the other had a clear boundary. On the unfenced playground, the children stayed close to their teacher, hesitant to venture too far. Meanwhile, at the fenced playground, the same group of children spread out, exploring freely within the space provided. The boundary didn't limit them; it empowered them to roam with confidence.

The same is true for teams. When leaders establish a clear vision—a north star everyone understands and believes in—

people move freely toward it in authentic, self-directed ways. There's no need for micromanagement. The path to that shared vision remains flexible and organic, guided by well-defined rules of engagement, supportive processes, and consistent check-ins that ensure alignment without stifling creativity. Within that framework, commitment and innovation can truly flourish.

> **When leaders establish a clear vision—a north star everyone understands and believes in—people move freely toward it in authentic, self-directed ways.**

A culture of commitment is always attuned to the dynamic expression of its core values. It doesn't set those values in stone and walk away. It revisits them regularly, not to rewrite or revise but to ensure they remain the right filters for decisions and behaviors. This ongoing reflection keeps the brand aligned, authentic, and relevant.

In this kind of culture, employees ask the hard, necessary questions:

- Does this still feel true to who we are?
- Are we living this value in the way we show up every day?
- How does this value guide our actions?

The focus isn't just on having values but on *living* them.

One of the most powerful aspects of a committed culture is how deeply invested people become. They embrace values and hold each other accountable to them. When the culture slips off course, the reckoning will usually come from within, not from the top. And while such a level of engagement can seem intense, perhaps even high maintenance, the truth is simple: emotional connection sparks emotional response. The leader's role is to harness that passion, channeling it in ways that elevate both the organization and the customer experience.

THE LISTENING TOUR

Listening is a critical component to creating a culture of commitment. I'm going to spend a lot of time on the topic of listening in Chapter 5 when I go deeper into connections. I want to bring up listening now as a way to help you understand whether you have a culture of commitment or a culture of compliance.

Over the years, as I've spent time meeting with and listening to employees, I've consistently sought clarity around a few key questions:

- Do they feel valued?
- How are they supported?
- What do they want, and why does it matter to them?
- What aren't they getting?
- What changes would be most meaningful?
- What small, immediate wins could make a difference right now?
- What could we be doing better?
- Where do they want us to go *together*?

Listening is a critical component to creating a culture of commitment.

If you're truly listening, the answers to these questions reveal more than just surface-level feedback. They tell you whether you're nurturing compliance or fostering commitment. Complaints, blame, and excuses? Those are signs of compliance. But suggestions, solutions, opinions, and even frustration are signs of engagement and belief. They signal that people *care* enough to speak up.

Remember, active listening is not about immediate response. You can take in all the data, find common themes, check your understanding, and move forward. That way, you solve for the right issues and move toward the right opportunities.

Curiosity and listening are incredible ways to build trust. They show people you are interested in and care about their opinions, concerns, and ideas.

WORKING GROUPS VS. TEAMS

There's a subtle but powerful difference between a group of people who work *together* and a team that's *truly connected*. It's the difference between compliance and commitment, and it starts with how you build, support, and lead any group.

A working group is often just a collection of individuals aligned by logistics, not belief. People show up, do their part, share information, and focus on their personal deliverables.

Accountability is individual. Goals are siloed. Roles are assigned. And while these groups can be efficient, they rarely tap into the deeper engagement or discretionary effort that drives transformation. At best, they produce solid work. At worst, they create burnout and disengagement.

A team on the other hand is a different kind of organism. In a true team, accountability is both individual and shared. People don't just care about their own output. They actually care about the *outcome*. They show up not only to deliver but to support, challenge, and co-create with one another. They meet frequently to solve problems, make decisions, plan, and reflect together.

Even defined roles are flexible. People step in, step up, and shift gears based on what the moment requires. That kind of adaptability comes from trust, not hierarchy. It's not accidental. It starts with the leader.

> **Curiosity and listening are incredible ways to build trust. They show people you are interested in and care about their opinions, concerns, and ideas.**

It's impossible to overstate the leader's role when shaping a team. Leaders have to move beyond delegation and performance reviews and become architects of culture and clarity. They must set the tone for what collaboration looks like, model the behaviors they want repeated, and most importantly, involve the team in defining "how," not just delivering on "what."

In a working group, purpose and process come from the top down. In a team, purpose (the "why") is something people co-create. The leader may chart the direction, but the team is there to shape the path. That shared authorship builds ownership, which creates commitment.

> **Leaders have to move beyond delegation and performance reviews and become architects of culture and clarity.**

Here's the truth: when people are merely assigned tasks, you get compliance. But when they feel connected to the mission, the team, and the impact, they commit. They show up not just with their hands but with their heads and their hearts. They challenge ideas, share responsibility, celebrate wins, and stay resilient when hard stuff happens. That's what turns performance into partnership.

So if you want more from your people, start by looking at what you're building: Are you managing a working group? Or are you leading a team? The difference isn't in the titles, but in the belief you cultivate and the commitment it earns.

NATURE ABHORS A VACUUM

Commitment or compliance. You choose. That's a simplification, but also a true undeniable fact. Cultures happen by design or default. When you don't translate belief into being an intentional and deliberate culture, then something else will fill that space. And it may not always be great.

When brands or leaders allow a culture of compliance to rule the day, employees will focus on reaching "good enough" but will never get to "great." A brand only gets on the path to greatness when it chooses to do so. Every brand has the potential to be great, but only very few brands achieve greatness. Why is that? It may not be because they don't want to be great. But it's a lot of work to be great, and it requires a level of commitment that can withstand explosive growth as well as meteoric failure. I believe that greatness requires clarity around the north star and leaders who possess a combination of passion, steadfastness, and adaptability in great abundance. It also requires teams with the same level of commitment. And that work sits squarely on the leader.

I firmly believe in the adage "Happy cows make happy

cheese," which I mentioned earlier. So, how do you create a legion of happy cows? If you're charged with leading a team, then you first have to believe that every member of your team has the potential for greatness. From there, you have to understand that it's your responsibility to provide the types of systems, strategies, resources, and support that empowers your people and the team as a whole to achieve greatness.

Commitment or compliance. You choose.
Cultures happen by design or default.

Once they make the choice to strive for greatness, it becomes your duty to cultivate an environment where success is possible and sustainable. True brand greatness doesn't come from a logo, a mission statement, or having the latest app. It comes from people. It always has, and it always will.

What's more, once you've unlocked the door to greatness through deep commitment, the next task becomes getting everyone to row in the same direction. How do you do that? Let's get into that next in Chapter 4.

*Before you create a culture where everyone
rows together, you have to codify your
mission, vision, and reason for being
to lock your north star into sight.*

CHAPTER 4

Rowing in the Same Direction

Building a culture of commitment means being committed to a bigger idea. Ideally, it also means that everyone is rowing in the same direction in order to achieve that idea. But that's not always the case. If some people are rowing this way but others row that way or only row when it suits them, then the boat will stay off track.

To be clear, when people row in different directions, it doesn't necessarily mean that they're actively trying to sabotage the goal or they want to force things according to their whim. More likely, it means there's misalignment somewhere. Everyone might be committed, but there's work to do before you can actualize their best collective effort and achieve transformative results.

When that's the case, leaders must go back to the source of misalignment and get people aligned with the bigger vision. If that means reinforcing *the why* behind a mission-driven project, then that's what you have to do.

It may also have to do with closing knowledge gaps, clarifying language, and clearing out any ambiguity that exists between feeling, meaning, and actions. No matter the case, leaders in these situations must be attuned to changes in synergy and alignment. They have to dive as deep as necessary to understand *why* misalignment exists in the first place. Then they have to focus on addressing the cause, not just the symptoms, in order to get the team on track.

CODIFICATION IS CRITICAL

When I introduced the topic of codification earlier, I mentioned how the actual process can be messy and emotional. That's why a lot of brands skip it. Here's the thing: before you create a culture where everyone rows together, you have to codify your mission, vision, and reason for being to lock your *north star* into sight.

This is much bigger than just creating a map that points to the north star. This work is about defining the actual destination itself. When you codify the truths of your brand, you are saying, "This is us. It's who we are and why we do things the way we do."

Everyone involved in building the brand must be clear on this vision, its breadth, and its full depth of meaning. This aligns with something I alluded to earlier: great brands know and appreciate the fact that they're not for everyone, nor do they need to be. Codifying your brand truths is another stake in the ground of this core belief.

Saying "This is us" is one way to get started, but actually nailing it down and codifying the "who we are" message is what moves the needle. That way, you're not just clarifying. You're also eliminating ambiguity.

Great brands understand this fundamental truth: they are not for everyone, nor do they need to be. The strongest brands embrace this, anchoring their identity in clear, unwavering principles. Codifying these brand truths is not just an exercise in self-definition; it's a declaration of purpose.

It's one thing to claim an identity, but truly defining and articulating who we are eliminates ambiguity and provides clarity that moves the needle.

Great brands understand this fundamental truth: they are not for everyone, nor do they need to be.

Words have a curious power. If I write "house," you'll picture one. But if I say "big house," your image sharpens. Add more detail—such as "big green house" or "big green house with white trim at the end of a quiet street"—and suddenly a scene takes shape. Yet even with this specificity, some details remain in your mind alone. Does the house have shutters? A manicured lawn? A basketball hoop in the driveway? A swimming pool in the backyard?

Precision matters. The clearer we are in defining our brand, the more vividly it comes to life for everyone who experiences it.

I've been a part of codifying missions, values, and brand truths at nearly every organization I've worked with. I've been tasked with creating concepts, tracking down meaning, revisiting old language, crowd-sourcing new language, and everything in between. It's really interesting and important work.

Here's something I've seen play out many times. First, a brand's well-established truths are nonetheless accidentally vague. To a large degree, everyone *loves* them—the sounds, the images they convey, the way they stack on a page of copy, etc. However, if you really press people, you discover that only a few of them actually possess complete clarity about what the words do and don't mean within the context of the brand experience.

This is an interesting dilemma from a Heart, Head, Hands perspective. If the words are full of feeling and everyone is on board from a heart-centered place, then what's the problem? Well, meaning is important, and when meaning is nebulous, you're setting up challenges.

Without codifying the actual meaning, those wonderful words that everyone *feels* will continue to be undefined. And, if you leave a space and ask people to fill it with their own meaning, then they will. When you have thousands of employees interpreting the core of who you are, it can and will create inconsistency, and perhaps even brand erosion.

So what do you do?

- First, make sure your north star is clear and that you have alignment where your brand's culture and values are concerned.
- Once you possess this clarity, double-down and define everything as clearly as possible. This isn't just a "we are" exercise but also a "we aren't" exercise. Go so far as to create examples, tell stories, and share experiences that reinforce the behaviors you want and illustrate the ones you don't.
- Remember, you'll want to engage in this process WITH employees. Nothing should feel like you're doing it TO them. You want buy-in through inclusion, not coercion.

Here are two of the great things that come out of doing this work up front. First, you create alignment. More importantly, you also create an environment where others bring their creativity, ideas, and solutions to helping you solve problems, identify opportunities, and move faster with better outcomes.

As a leader, your job isn't to have all the answers. It's to create the conditions for the answers to come from everyone around you. In other words, it's to unleash the potential in your teams.

WHAT ROWING TOGETHER LOOKS LIKE

When I was regional director for Gap's Boston region, I oversaw sixty stores and nearly a thousand employees. I also witnessed firsthand the brand's dramatic shift. Once the darling of Wall Street, Gap could do no wrong...until it could do nothing right.

Sales declined steadily, the result of decisions that strayed from our core customer. In pursuit of a new audience that had little interest in us, we alienated the loyal shoppers who had defined our success. This misstep created a void of our own making, leaving us struggling to reclaim what we had lost.

> **As a leader, your job isn't to have all the answers. It's to create the conditions for the answers to come from everyone around you.**

As anyone in a declining business knows firsthand, what followed was a combination of panic and short-term decisions to try to stop the bleeding. By then, Gap had been doing everything differently. We slashed costs, mainly payroll, in order to shore things up. We were making decisions to try to operate ourselves out of the descent but not focus on how to address the bigger issue of why our customers didn't want to shop with us anymore.

My team and I—there were ten district managers—met and decided to at least try to answer this very basic question: how do we turn this around? Right away we discovered that to get that answer, we needed to answer two other questions: how did we get here, and what's preventing us from driving business forward?

We laid everything on the table amongst ourselves, discussed the way things had been back when everything was going well, and focused on some of the critical decisions that had knocked the brand off course. We included the store management teams and employees to get insight as well as test assumptions and hypotheses that we were creating.

When we finally came back to our starting question, we decided that what was missing was something Gap had been a leader in for years, something I referred to as "clarity of offering." Our customer wanted to know what we believed in, the big ideas, the trends and create a shopping experience that was easy and fun, not chaotic. And the way we do that for men, women, and children is different. That meant we needed to revisit and redefine our way of merchandising—a complete tear-down, followed by a rebuild.

From there, we went into action. If we were going to rethink how we showed up for the customer, we needed to get the people who knew the customer best involved.

We gathered up all the merchants from each store, key general managers, district managers, plus our head regional merchant, and took a road trip to Vermont. There was such an incredible energy around this, and it was not only important work, but it was such an incredible example of commitment and teamwork that it still resonates as one of the most powerful experiences I had in my career. It wasn't easy and definitely wasn't a vacation.

We had no budget, and with sales slumping as they were, we had no money to do any of this. But we were a scrappy group and figured out how to make it work—because we all knew how important it was to our survival as a brand. Instead of letting obstacles get in the way, we stayed curious and got creative.

We took over the store in Burlington and worked two overnight shifts once the store was closed. Both nights, we broke into teams and focused on a specific section of the store. We had some basic tenets that described what we were trying to accomplish with regards to merchandising and customer journeys, but overall, each team had creative freedom to design their section in whatever way they thought best. This is a great example of the "freedom within a framework" philosophy I love so much.

In the morning, each group walked the rest of us through what they'd done, explaining the thinking behind their ideas. Then we'd all talk through various pros and cons of what we saw, take notes, make adjustments, and move to the next group.

Once we finished this exercise, we walked away with an entirely new merchandising strategy that we felt could really improve the customer experience and, ultimately, results. The only problem was this: because of payroll issues and staffing cuts, we weren't equipped to re-merchandise and sell in every store in our region. But we still needed to prove that our strategy could work.

Once again we brought our entire team into the conversation to get their ideas and buy-in, and together we came up with a solution. Instead of all sixty stores, we would focus on twelve. And every store in the region would try to give a couple hours of their already reduced payroll to help us fully staff each of the twelve stores. We knew the strategy would only work if we were able to sell our way out of the problem.

Staying with these twelve stores, we held daily conference calls with managers to see how things were going, find out what they'd done, and to get a sense of what they were seeing and experiencing. We weren't just sitting back in our ivory tower, so to speak, waiting for the magic to happen on its own. We made this a living, breathing learning environment where we were open about challenges and failures, shared successes and best practices, and adjusted in real time based on what we found. It was stressful and frustrating and invigorating!

Here's what we discovered. In two weeks, the stores where we implemented changes started picking up momentum. If the region was down 40 percent, then these stores were only down 20 percent. Two weeks after that, they were only down 10 percent. Finally, they flattened out. By then, these stores were easily outpacing other stores from across our region and the company.

It was working. There were a couple of fundamental reasons why these stores became more successful. In essence, our group was super clear on these critical points: what we were solving for and where we were starting from.

Many times, brands and their leaders like to wax poetic about the future, the vision, and the utopian state of the world to come, but they don't have the appetite for digging under the covers to provide an objective, fact-based assessment of where they currently are. If the above two points don't work in tandem, you will never be able to see the way forward, let alone create it.

Here's a personal example that highlights how a lack of clarity can leave you circling. Back when I was at Apple, I not only oversaw stores in North America but, for a time, Europe as well. During this period, I would travel nonstop. During one particular stretch, I went from working in London to flying to Cupertino, California, for meetings, then catching a red-eye to Washington, DC, for a store event.

As you can imagine, it was a ton of flying in a short amount of time. I was exhausted, slightly disoriented, and far from the top of my game.

I rented a car in Dulles Airport and started driving to my

hotel so I could shower and change before going to the store event. I don't know how familiar you are with traffic in and around Dulles, but let's just say that within ten minutes I was so confused that I was still trying to do something other than circling the airport, which is what was happening. This was before things like Google Maps and Waze. It was me and my trusty MapQuest printout against the world.

I was too tired to figure things out and had no idea where I was. I called the hotel hoping they could help. The very kind gentleman on the other end of the phone, hearing my frustration, said "I can absolutely help you get here...I just need to know where you are."

If I was in a better state of mind, I might have just chuckled. But being sleep-deprived and double jet-lagged, I snapped.

"I have no idea where I'm at. That's the problem!"

The reality: if you don't know where you are starting from, you can't get directions to where you want to go. Even more to the point: you certainly can't create a situation where you can successfully direct or orchestrate a team to make it happen. You have to be clear about your reality. It's critical to moving toward your ideal outcome.

Let me bring things back to the Gap story now. Something else...something *extra*...drove our work, ideas, and execution. In fact, this *thing* made the entire strategy come to life. It was the fact that the mandate driving these changes came from a gathering of people at the store, district, and management level working together. It was not from the top down or a dusty playbook or some third-party consultancy that said "do this/get that." It was a collective response that coalesced around solving a challenge. People from all these different areas jumped on board and quickly began rowing together.

**If you don't know where you are
starting from, you can't get directions
to where you are going.**

Our business improved because we established absolute clarity around expectations. Everyone understood the problem we were trying to solve. We weren't just aiming to turn things around for the sake of our jobs. We were fighting to revive a once-beloved brand.

To do so, we created an environment where the best ideas came from those on the front lines—the people who lived the work every day. This wasn't about me as the leader issuing top-down mandates from behind a desk. Instead, we built a process rooted in consensus, bringing together the right mix of voices from every level of the organization. We crowdsourced solutions, collaborated as a team, and ensured that everyone in the room had a seat and a say.

As I wrote above, everyone knew what was at stake. My role, above all, was to be clear, honest, and transparent. There was no point in sugarcoating the obvious. They deserved the truth, not platitudes. I needed to treat them not just as employees but as adults who shared in both the challenge and the responsibility of our success.

Now, if you're waiting to find out how our *little engine that could* story played out across the Gap brand, I'll cut right to the chase: it didn't scale. It's not that people didn't listen. They did. The brand even tried to put a playbook together. It's just...well, they tried in a very "compliance-minded" way. Here's what I mean.

Our numbers kept getting better and better to the point where we drew some positive attention from senior leadership. I met with the executive vice president of stores and explained what we were doing. By the end of the meeting, we shared excitement and hope that other regions could do this as well. The executive vice president picked four other regions across the country to go and try the same approach. Sadly, they didn't experience the same results.

What was missing? It's easy to play Monday Morning Quarterback, but when I reflected on it, one thing that was missing was the energy that existed in our region when we created it. We'd built a working culture of commitment, collaboration, inclusion, and engagement. In fact, we'd put this culture into place well before our trip to Vermont. Our team was already working as a collective, so when we had to take action, the foundation was already in place. We were working in a Heart, Head, Hands fashion: we rode the wave of our collective belief into creating strategy, then committed to executing on it.

I'm not a huge sports analogy guy (despite writing "Monday Morning Quarterback" one paragraph ago), but here's one: championship teams know how to play together before they go into "the big game." Nothing happens by accident or on the fly. These teams prepare long before the whistle blows—honing their skills, refining their teamwork, and solidifying their plan. This level of preparation ensures that when the moment comes, they're not just reacting randomly; they're responding with confidence, always ready to pivot, adjust, and ultimately succeed.

EMPOWERING DOES NOT MEAN ABANDONING

When I mention "rowing in the same direction," I don't mean building a ship without a captain. Far from it. Leadership isn't about stepping aside. It's about showing up. There's a world of difference between empowering employees and abandoning them. Without an engaged leader guiding the process, real change simply can't happen.

When you ask how transformation occurs, the truth is, it starts at the top. A team can rally, employees can advocate for change, and the energy for something new can build like fire, but ultimately, leaders make the call.

Leadership isn't about stepping aside. It's about showing up. There's a world of difference between empowering employees and abandoning them.

When people are aligned with a clear vision, and when they truly understand what we're trying to achieve as a team and as a brand, it unlocks something powerful. Suddenly, floodgates open. The energy behind questions changes. Gone is a question like "Why are we even doing this?" In its place you hear "Can we *really* try this?" A statement like "They won't let us do this" becomes "What if we did it this way?"

That's when real momentum begins.

I emphasized in Chapter 2 that your employees are a company's greatest asset. They are literally your "secret sauce." Let's unpack this.

To start, they are the ones who bring your business to life, shaping every customer interaction. That's not just true for front-line workers. It includes everyone, from those crafting vision and strategy to the people who manage data, develop products, build marketing campaigns, develop talent, oversee finances, and on and on. At its core, every organization, whether five or fifty-thousand employees strong, is powered by people.

No leader can oversee every action, nor should they. In a committed environment, leadership shifts from control to inspiration. When your team is aligned, your role evolves. You become a guide, offering perspective, tools, and resources that empower them to take on greater, more meaningful challenges. And in doing so you are developing the leaders of the future.

I am a huge believer in the idea that says, "Do the job only you can do." As a leader you have to figure out what that is for you and your people. If there is a job and you know someone else can do it, give it to them.

> **In a committed environment, leadership shifts from control to inspiration. When your team is aligned, your role evolves.**

A former boss of mine, from way back when I was an assistant buyer at May Co., gave me advice I still think about today. I was leaving for my rotation as a department manager in stores. He said, "Your job is ultimately to do nothing." I was twenty-two years old at the time. It sounded like the best job ever. However, as it sank in I realized that in order for me to actually do *nothing*, everyone who worked for or with me would have to be able to do my job. So my real goal as a leader wasn't about abandoning them...it was about developing them.

Message received!

What does this type of development look like? Are there steps? Tools? Tips and tricks to speed it up and move it along? Anyone can enforce rules. But how do we cultivate belief and buy-in?

We're going to go deeper and answer these in Part 2 as we explore the CADET framework I wrote about at the start. And it all begins with how you connect with your people.

Part 2

When you consistently connect with others, you create the foundation for meaningful, lasting change through authentic and deep relationships.

CHAPTER 5

Connect

LISTEN TO UNDERSTAND

Sometimes a single connection can feel small or even insignificant. Over time, those moments add up and create trust, understanding, alignment, and momentum.

When you consistently connect with others, you create the foundation for meaningful, lasting change through authentic and deep relationships. It might not feel revolutionary at the moment, but connection is what drives transformation. Personally and professionally, it's what I value most. I truly can't stress enough how important it is.

I believe connecting with people is the most critical link between belief and commitment. In Chapter 1, I asked you to delve into what you believe about your brand and how your brand manifests its beliefs. Here I'll ask a similar and equally important question. What do your people believe: about the brand, the work, and their role in it?

You won't find these answers in policies or metrics. The only way to get them is to connect with your people: to invest the effort to learn and to seek to understand before being understood.

Many leaders are quick to dive into action. The results are driving them, and urgency is their fuel. When you skip connection, you miss the foundation that gives strategy its meaning. Remember, true impact doesn't begin with doing. It begins with understanding. That's how you see the bigger picture—and bring others along with you.

When I was leading teams, one of my biggest fears was being out of touch with the reality of what was happening in the business, with our employees, and with our customers. I was worried that the decisions we were making at the highest levels regarding direction, strategy, and execution were disconnected from what we really needed.

When you skip connection, you miss the foundation that gives strategy its meaning.

I'm sure we've all heard a phrase similar to "decisions made in the ivory tower." It exists for a reason. When leaders are too removed from the day-to-day reality, the decisions they make miss the mark.

I used to have the following fear: I would be on a conference call with ten thousand employees talking about a new initiative or giving directions we wanted people to execute on. Meanwhile, on the other end of the phone (this is way before video calls) people would be rolling their eyes, looking at each other, and asking things like "Does he even know what we deal with on a daily basis?" or "When was the last time he asked us what we need or think?"

I believe the most powerful direction comes from a dynamic

exchange where top-down vision meets bottom-up insight. When leaders stay connected with their people, we do more than gather information. We unlock understanding, spark ideas, and co-create decisions that move everyone forward. Without that connection, we're leading in the dark.

CREATING CONDITIONS FOR CONNECTION

There's no single framework for connection and no rulebook to follow. But most of us share a need to connect in ways that genuinely resonate with others. While your approach will naturally reflect your own style and organizational reality, whether you interact daily, rely on impromptu chats, navigate across time zones, or something else, what matters most isn't *how* you connect but *why* you do so.

> I believe the most powerful direction comes from a dynamic exchange where top-down vision meets bottom-up insight.

What's the most crucial mindset to have when it comes to creating an authentic connection? Curiosity. In fact, I believe curiosity is the most powerful tool we have in any conversation. Yet it's also the one we most often forget to use.

Prioritizing connection begins with intentionally creating the conditions for it. This is where actionable insight, the kind that drives alignment, sharpens strategy, and advances a brand's vision, comes into being.

Whether you're assessing engagement, identifying friction points, or surfacing unmet needs, authentic connection offers a clear read on how people experience the brand internally. This goes beyond intention and gets to the heart of how people actually *feel*.

I used to believe that the primary purpose of connecting with others was to gather as many perspectives as possible. That's one of the reasons, but I've come to realize it's actually a secondary goal. The first and far more important goal is to signal that you're present, available, and genuinely interested. That you're truly *listening*.

GAINING PERSPECTIVES

When you hear from other people, you're essentially finding out how they understand, feel, and think about your brand. What's working? What isn't? What needs to change? What ideas have we not even thought of as it relates to improving the brand?

This isn't just about letting people vent (though some might). It's about gaining insight, identifying blind spots, and generating ideas to help you challenge and perhaps even refine your own understanding of the brand. In the end, you're looking for the most authentic feedback you can get, even if and when it's emotionally charged.

On that note, don't shy away from the emotions that surface during meaningful connection. One of the most important lessons I've learned is that when you create safe spaces for people to share, vulnerability naturally emerges. Within that vulnerability lies truth. How you respond to that truth—whether with openness or defensiveness—can determine if trust takes root.

Rather than resisting it, lean in. If you want people to offer honest feedback about the brand, they might not feel safe at first. They need to know their feelings are welcome, that their voices matter, and that there are no wrong answers.

When you create safe spaces for people to share, vulnerability naturally emerges. Within that vulnerability lies truth.

Equally important is understanding the source of their emotions. Are they excited by untapped potential? Are they signaling that something's broken? Has something they once deeply valued gone away? Is something ready for change? Often, these moments offer a window into new opportunities to explore or paradigms that need to shift. This is where connection begins to blur into assessment—two leadership behaviors that rarely happen in isolation. As you build more connections, you're also gathering insight, context, and clarity. What you'll find is that the two move naturally in tandem.

With that said, it's vital to stay aware of your own filters. Confirmation bias has a subtle way of shaping what we hear. Ask yourself often: *Am I truly listening? Or am I reshaping their words to align with what I already believe?* Genuine connection requires presence, humility, and the courage to be changed by what you learn.

As you build more connections, you're also gathering insight, context, and clarity.

ACTIVE LISTENING

Effective connection is all about active listening, which gains its fuel from curiosity. Ultimately, active listening is the foundation of every connection you make and foster. It's where understanding begins and where solutions take hold.

Leaders who prioritize active listening create environments where employees feel valued and empowered. It is also the only way to ensure clarity, which is critical for alignment.

Genuine connection requires presence, humility, and the courage to be changed by what you learn.

Active listening is a type of listening that digs into how people feel and what they think. This kind of listening doesn't come with judgment, nor is it a fishing expedition where you're trying to validate your own opinion. It's about gathering perspectives and gaining insight.

Much like curiosity itself, active listening is a rare and undervalued art. I often think of it on a scale from –5 to +5. At –5, you're simply waiting for your turn to speak. You know...talking over others, finishing their sentences, or mentally rehearsing your reply. But what happens at +5? That's when you're fully engaged. You're "listening with the willingness to be altered."

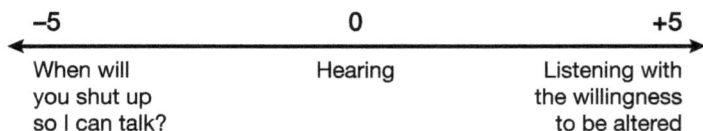

–5	0	+5
When will you shut up so I can talk?	Hearing	Listening with the willingness to be altered

That phrase *listening with the willingness to be altered* is one of my favorites. Imagine entering a conversation with your own opinions yet being open and curious enough to let what you hear reshape what you think. This is the type and level of listening I'm talking about.

Connecting through listening isn't a strategy in my mind. It's a way of being. It may also be the literal embodiment of the commitment we're trying to build. Connecting through listening says you hear people, you recognize them as individuals, and that to you, every voice matters. It fosters a culture of trust, collaboration, and belief. It's a vital step toward transforming teams, organizations, and, ultimately, results.

I've been working on this type of listening for decades. I won't pretend I've mastered it. It's hard. But I keep trying. Because I still believe it's the only way forward.

ASKING THE RIGHT QUESTIONS

The art of listening involves asking the right questions. I'm sure like me, perhaps you've gone through training on asking open- and closed-ended questions. Open-ended questions invite deeper reflection and meaningful dialogue, unlike closed-ended questions, which can be answered with a simple "yes" or "no."

Open-ended questions encourage people to elaborate, explore their thoughts, and share their experiences. While this approach often requires more time, it's in these longer, more thoughtful responses that we begin to uncover what truly matters.

To that end, I am a huge fan of *The 5 Whys* line of questioning. When someone gives you their first answer, don't stop there. Ask a version of "Why is that?" or "Can you tell me more?"

Each answer brings you closer to the truth. Too often, we rush to solve the first thing we hear, addressing symptoms rather than the cause. Only after we understand the real opportunities and issues are we equipped to solve the right problem—and create solutions that last.

When I was leading teams, regardless of whether I was starting fresh with a new organization, moving to an existing team, or hiring new team members, one of the first things I'd do was ask everyone to fill out what I jokingly referred to as their "owner's manual." Believe it or not, this simple document helped to supercharge the connection phase of building a relationship.

After people filled it out, we would have a one-hour touch-base meeting. During the first thirty minutes, employees would share what they wrote, and I would ask clarifying questions to understand.

The second half of our meeting was for me to share my personal owner's manual and for them to ask questions. This was a fun and productive way to start the process of learning how to be the best leader for them. In short, it was a chance to understand more about them while also (I hope) giving them useful insight into how I showed up, viewed the world, and from where I drew my expectations.

Below you'll find the list of questions and conversation starters I would share. These aren't meant as the *be all and end all* of the questions you can ask. Some of them aren't even written as questions. You may have your own questions or statements that you already use. They might be way better than what I'm sharing below. If so, that's great!

I'm sharing these as a way to illustrate a very important point: the intentional, deliberate effort you put into making connections is important but doesn't have to be tricky or complicated.

All About Me: An Owner's Manual

- Background information, such as school, previous experiences...

- My most satisfying accomplishments are...
- What motivates me?
- My ideal type of work: activities that energize me are...
- Where and how I make my greatest contribution are...
- This is how I measure my success...
- How I measure other's success...
- How I like to learn, assess, and make decisions...
- What keeps me up at night?
- How to get the best from me in meetings?
- Here's what I need from you to get the most out of our time together...
- What to do when we disagree?
- What irritates me?
- When I need you to push back...
- When it's best to leave me alone...
- Things that confuse people about my behavior (at least that I know of)...
- How to and when to give me feedback...
- Any other important information you should know about me...

CHECKING FOR UNDERSTANDING

Checking for understanding is another important part of asking the right questions. How many times have we heard what someone said yet interpreted it incorrectly or filled in blanks with our own version of ideas or biases?

Few things make people feel more seen and respected than knowing that you've made the effort to understand them as they intended. The opposite is also true. People feel disrespected or completely unvalued if you simply take their words and apply your own meaning to them.

One way to avoid this, and to ensure that you are hearing and interpreting them correctly, is to rephrase and repeat back to them what you've heard, adding context where necessary.

Few things make people feel more seen and respected than knowing that you've made the effort to understand them as they intended.

For instance, leading with something as simple as "So let me make sure I understand...what I heard you say is..." allows them to either confirm you're correct or redirect you. Either way, the job of this type of back and forth is to ensure that you both understand. It gives the other person power over their words and gives you clarity. This isn't just a communication tactic; it forms alignment and trust, two of the most valuable outcomes of intentional listening.

LISTENING BEYOND WORDS

Active listening involves what you're hearing, but it goes beyond that as well. As best you can, you also have to pay attention to tone, body language, and the context in which someone shares something.

A person's nonverbal cues tell so much about what they are really feeling and thinking. I have always thought about this as the meaning between the words. And as a leader you need to be 100 percent present in the conversation to pick up on it. The reality is, being truly present is like listening at a +5 all the time. Yes, it's really hard, but aren't the most important things in life worth the extra work?

CONNECTING MEANS COMMITMENT

Connecting isn't a one-and-done activity. It's an ongoing commitment. It requires time, energy, and consistency. For a leader, that means showing up even when it's inconvenient and continuing to be present. It also means being as vulnerable and honest as you want other people to be. Leading means going first, being the example, and demonstrating behavior.

Here's a concept I'd like you to consider. At the start of this chapter I mentioned the critical link between belief and commitment, and referenced the question I asked in Chapter 1: what do you believe about your brand? Then I asked what do your people believe about the brand, the work, and their role in it?

> Connecting isn't a one-and-done activity. It's an ongoing commitment. It requires time, energy, and consistency.

Now it's time for another round of questions along these same lines: First, what do you believe about the role of connection in cultivating true commitment? Second, how comfortable are you with exhibiting the level of vulnerability and intention that true connection requires?

Here's the truth: if the idea of genuine connection edges you out of your comfort zone, that's not a cue to pull back but a prompt to go deeper.

Because before you can connect with others meaningfully, you need clarity on **why** you're choosing to connect in the first place.

This isn't about being overly soft or sentimental. It's about understanding how to meaningfully influence the organization.

That's why I call connection the Holy Grail for any brand steward. When you stand with your people, and when they know you're truly with them, they'll walk with you. And when that alignment exists, you can create shared moments, harness collective energy, and move forward together toward a unified vision.

Once connecting becomes a regular and recognized habit, you'll see noticeable shifts in your culture. That's what happens when people know you're hearing them. It's a powerful message that says, "You matter." When employees hear this message, they're more likely to buy into the company's vision, especially when it aligns with their own.

Connection is just the beginning. It's a powerful and transformative starting point that provides the clarity, insight, and context needed to make informed decisions. But connection alone isn't enough. What follows is just as critical: assessment.

If connections give you powerful insights into what matters, what's working, and where the gaps are, then assessment turns those insights into strategy. It's the process of translating what you've heard into actionable direction, guiding the path forward toward a brand vision that is not only scalable but sustainable and profitable. With connection as your compass and assessment as your map, you can align people, priorities, and performance.

It's time to talk about the role that assessment plays in shaping the outcomes you're striving for.

When you assess, you effectively build the bridge between understanding and action. That's how you turn what you've heard into a clear path you'll follow when it's time to deliver.

CHAPTER 6

Assess

STRATEGIZE AND DEEPEN TRUST

Assessing comes from the desire to find solutions to the bigger goal of transforming experiences, relationships, and results. While connection is all about listening and learning, assessing is about putting what you've learned to work.

If you've been connecting with people and really listening to them, then you've also been gathering information, knowledge, and insights. Maybe you've begun to discover new ways to get them interested and engaged in what's happening with your organization. You might have even uncovered some hard truths about what's working, what isn't, and what's in your wheelhouse as far as change goes. This is all great! Now what? How will you put these insights to work in a way that creates change and perhaps transforms experiences? That's where assessing comes in.

TRANSLATE INSIGHTS BEFORE TAKING ACTIONS

Assessing is the link that ties all of your connections together. It's the convergence of understanding what people want (stated and unstated) and matching their wants with what you can actually offer (existing or developed). It's the strategy piece that involves taking the truth or truths you've heard and using them to shape a collective vision people can rally behind.

When you assess, you effectively build the bridge between understanding and action. That's how you turn what you've heard into a clear path you'll follow when it's time to deliver. It's how you make sure you're moving toward the right solutions and how you align your entire inventory of options as you aim toward relevant, intentional actions.

Assessment is a lot like building a strategic map. Through the process, you identify where you are, clarify what resources and capabilities you have in place, make note of what's missing, and ensure that all team members who are on the journey feel relevant and focused.

Sometimes what emerges from assessment is surprisingly practical. Let's say you went on a listening tour. Your goal was to figure out why morale was so low. You set your biases aside and went about the work of connecting. Now that you've gathered your input, some interesting correlations start to emerge.

You've discovered that the brand's culture isn't the issue. It's literally the physical workplace environment. People shared with you that "the stores are cold and poorly lit," "the break rooms are a mess," "the bathrooms are never picked up," "the HVAC is haunted," and other gems. Do these employees need a pizza party? Not at all. What they actually need is better lighting, a new facilities partner, and an HVAC upgrade. None of these updates are grand gestures, but each one is meaningful. Individually and as a group, they show your people that you're listening.

Other times, needs that emerge when you assess are operational in nature. Maybe you need to invest in more training based on customer net promoter scores (NPS) about product knowledge. However, employees lack time for more conventional off-the-floor classroom sessions.

With their input, you design short, shift-friendly microlearnings instead of long-form modules. It's a tailored solution. First, you listened, then you refined through assessment. From there, you aligned to outcomes. More about that in a moment.

No matter what situation you're in, three things come to mind when I think of assessment:

1. How you direct your focus on what matters and what's within reach can shape relationships, expectations, and long-term trust. Small decisions have an outsized impact when people feel seen, heard, and valued.
2. Your ability to translate feedback into a clear direction is crucial. A compelling vision means little if it fails to reflect the lived experience of your people or misses their spoken and unspoken needs.
3. Assessment allows you to understand where employee expectations may be out of line with the brand's identity or direction. This awareness is critical. It gives you the opportunity to either realign people and the brand or acknowledge when they may not be the right fit for one another and help them find a place they will be happier.

A compelling vision means little if it fails to reflect the lived experience of your people or misses their spoken and unspoken needs.

THE TRUST FACTOR

In Chapter 5, I mentioned that connecting and assessing usually work hand in hand. When you're connecting, you're gathering insights. Assessing is the point where insights begin to fold into plans. Trust is something both steps have in common.

Let's look at things this way. When you connect, you're opening doors. While you're assessing, you're exploring what to do with what you learned inside those open doors, what has to change, improve, or be created in order to move forward.

Taking things further, identifying the opportunities is just the start. You also have to understand the scope, have a clear grasp on the present state, be able to build the path from reality to the ideal state, and know how to lean on your people as you look for the solution. To lead in this way is to see around corners.

In the end, trust is fragile and fleeting. It doesn't just compound interest in a dusty vault. You have to continue to build on it. To help do so, keep this in mind: if you misidentify a problem, overpromise a solution, or miss the mark completely and sink back into your own confirmation bias, then any trust you've built will erode. Worse, instead of going back to zero, the trust factor will most likely slip into the negative, especially if people feel like you've pulled the rug out from under them or didn't listen to them in good faith.

COLLABORATION, NOT ISOLATION

Part of being on a team where trust matters involves being able to leverage the talents and strengths of every person. There is a quote from Marcus Buckingham I love and use quite often: "The team is well-rounded, precisely because the individuals aren't." Don't you love it? The notion: the very thing that makes a team powerful is the uniqueness of each person on it.

This same concept can help you as a leader create meaningful, effective strategies and solutions. Include your people and their talents in the process. Give them voice and agency as they take in the vision. Let them know what the current reality is. Remind them that you'll be working together to create ideas, plans, and actions. Reinforce the fact that they're a part of deciding what your north star is. Then give them the tools and support they need as the whole brand moves closer to it.

Of the many times I've seen top-down direction fail, it usually came down to one of three reasons: (1) it didn't solve for what was really happening, (2) resources were not aligned to expectations, or (3) employees didn't embrace it because they weren't committed to the ideas or vision. I want to spend a little time discussing the third reason.

When employees have no skin in the game, it becomes a crapshoot as to who embraces direction and who doesn't. Don't mistake this for the inmates running the asylum or death by committee. I'm talking about something completely different: strategic collaboration and representation.

For leaders, this means realizing that the best ideas don't always reside in the *ivory tower*, which I mentioned in Chapter 5. In fact, they rarely do. However, when you tap into the collective genius of teams and organization, when you create the conditions for working together, the sum will prove to be greater than the parts.

When employees have no skin in the game, it becomes a crapshoot as to who embraces direction and who doesn't.

That said, not every decision, plan, or solution needs to emerge from group consensus. You have to have a clear structure for collaboration and engagement that prioritizes alignment over agreement. When that's in place, your strategies will reflect the best thinking of the brand, not just the loudest voices in the room.

> **You have to have a clear structure for collaboration and engagement that prioritizes alignment over agreement.**

Here are two professional examples of what can happen when intentional connection feeds into the power of open-minded assessments.

LEARNING AS YOU GO

Years ago, I was leading Apple's North American retail organization during a period of explosive growth. The brand was opening fifty stores a year. We were scaling from ten thousand to twenty-five thousand employees over a three year time period. As it was happening, one insight became crystal clear from the net promoter feedback we'd gathered: our product knowledge wasn't where it needed to be.

Back then, 90 percent of customers walked into our stores having already researched Apple products online. That meant our teams needed to meet or exceed their level of knowledge in order to earn credibility and build trust. To do so, employees needed more training and learning opportunities to increase product knowledge. The problem: if you've visited an Apple store, you know how busy they can be. Back then when there were fewer stores, they were even busier.

When we started discussing how to upskill employees, the initial response to any kind of traditional classroom-based training was an emphatic *no*. Their pushback was pretty direct: "There's no time...everyone's always busy...we don't have the space or resources for that." Every concern was valid...at least on the surface.

I went back to my team and asked them a simple but important question: "Are you saying that every employee is actively engaged, without pause, for the full eight hours of every shift?"

This sparked some curiosity. The team went out, spoke with employees, gathered insights, and came back with a key realization: while days were busy, *everyone* had pockets of downtime—around thirty minutes per day, though not all at once.

We took this new information and reframed the challenge, using what we knew from the connect phase to inform how we assessed. We broke things down like this:

- What do employees actually need?
- What does their day really look like?
- What tools do we already have?
- What can we create to make learning practical and effective?

I thought back to the SRA cards I used in elementary school. If you're not familiar, it was a self-paced, self-directed reading program. You'd read a card, take a quick quiz to check comprehension, pass, then move on. Believe it or not, this concept became our inspiration.

We built our own version of SRA cards: modular, on-the-floor learning that employees could engage with in short bursts, guided by peer coaches and buddies. No classrooms. No scheduling conflicts. Just smart, accessible learning in the flow of work.

Within six months, we saw a .6-point increase in product knowledge NPS. This was an extraordinary jump. Just as importantly, our employees grew in confidence through competence.

It was also a powerful reminder that when you understand the reality of your environment (connecting) and meet people where they are with approaches and resources that are relevant (assessing), solutions don't have to be complicated to be effective. They just have to be intentional.

BUILDING FROM WITHIN

My second story is set in 2013, when I was leading the global retail business at Tory Burch. We identified that one of the most impactful ways to drive business growth was to strengthen our *clienteling* strategy. We saw an opportunity to leverage emerging technology to create a system that would empower teams to build deeper, more personalized relationships with customers.

We initially partnered with an external vendor to bring this vision to life. It quickly became clear that the software they had promised wasn't ready and wouldn't be for quite some time. Rather than wait, we made the decision to co-develop the solution internally, in close partnership with the vendor.

The first step I took as a leader was to assemble the right project team. I wanted to go beyond the usual suspects from IT, corporate, and e-commerce and include the people who would actually be using the tool day in and day out. With that in mind, our team included general managers, assistant managers, sales associates, and even stock team members. In other words, the employees who were closest to customers. They knew what mattered and what didn't when it came to building a lasting client relationship.

Their insights were our secret weapon. Because they helped

shape the design and functionality of our new tool from the ground up, we ended up creating a best-in-class clienteling system. More than just work, it made everyone's jobs easier. Most importantly, teams from across the organization adopted it because it was intuitive, practical, and directly aligned with their needs. When they used it, they showed up as rock stars for customers.

And the best part? The process never ended. We treated the system as a living product. We constantly gathered feedback from users and partners and asked what they loved, what they struggled with, and what they needed next. That continuous loop of listening and evolving kept the tool relevant, useful, and always improving.

RESILIENCE THROUGH ASSESSMENT

When leaders and, ideally, entire organizations embrace assessment as an ongoing discipline, they do far more than solve problems. They cultivate resilience. They foster a culture where feedback isn't feared but welcomed as a vital tool for learning and growth.

In these environments, people are empowered to identify challenges and also address them in real time, often before they escalate. This is the foundation of a true learning culture: one where mistakes aren't hidden out of fear but seen as opportunities to learn, evolve, and improve.

Incentives play a critical role in shaping that type of culture. When we introduced NPS to my organization, I made a clear decision: compensation would not be directly tied to NPS results. Why? Because pressure to perform against a number often leads to manipulation rather than meaningful insight.

Think about what happens when you buy a car and the salesperson urges you to give all 10s on the survey...because their bonus depends on it. Few customers want to penalize someone's paycheck, even if their experience wasn't great. The result? A distorted view of the customer journey and a missed opportunity to improve.

Our goal wasn't to chase scores but to create truly transformational experiences. To do that, we needed honest feedback. And we needed employees to feel safe enough to embrace that feedback without financial consequence. Our mantra was simple, powerful, and straight ahead: *we may not always get it right, but we will always make it right.*

That shift changed everything. Teams became deeply invested in the feedback. Within twenty-four hours of receiving a detractor comment, we reached out personally. Our goal wasn't to defend but to understand and make things right.

Customers were often stunned, both by the fact that we actually read and responded to their feedback and that we actually cared enough to address the issues. The experience alone often turned dissatisfaction into loyalty.

Our leaders came to love this part of their jobs. So much so that over time, teams even began reaching out to passives and promoters as well. They were energized by the act of listening, learning, and creating moments that mattered. They wanted to go beyond *meeting* expectations and had their eyes on exceeding them. And they did, through connection, assessment, and a deep commitment to transformation.

Let me pause on the topic of transformation before we get ahead of ourselves. I'll come back to it in Chapter 9. I want to share two more stories about assessment in action.

THE CONVERGENCE OF CONNECTING
AND ASSESSING

Remember my Gap story from Chapter 4, where a group of merchants, general managers, district managers, and our head regional merchant took off for Vermont to save the brand? That was about the power of rowing together. The story I'm about to share has more to do with the assessment piece of the puzzle.

It was during that same era for the brand, when we were down negative double-digit comps every day. As part of Gap's response, they pulled together a cross-functional group of us, took us out of position, and gave us the task of leading a high-priority initiative aimed at reimagining the brand from the inside out.

We didn't jump into any preconceived notions or biases. Instead, we started with the goal of deeply understanding our customers both demographically and, more importantly, psychographically. We explored their values, motivations, and aspirations in order to form a more meaningful connection. After we gained that clarity, we moved into assessment: examining every aspect of the customer experience, including store design, layout, product assortment, marketing strategy, selling approach, and operational model.

After that, we put our strategy into action: we closed nine stores in a test market and fully implemented the redesigned experience. The initial results were remarkable, both in performance and customer feedback. The concept really resonated with people, and the momentum was real.

Unfortunately, despite the success of this pilot, the brand wasn't able to transform at scale on account of a range of structural and operational challenges. It was disappointing, but the experience reinforced a few things:

1. First: meaningful connection is a prerequisite to designing meaningful experiences. You must understand your customer *before* you build for them.
2. Second: assessment must precede action, and the quality of that assessment is directly tied to the diversity of perspectives informing it. Our team brought together voices from across the organization, including every major function critical to turning the north star into reality.
3. Third: the experience brought home the importance of aligning insight, strategy, and execution in a way that is both human-centered and operationally sound.

> **Assessment must precede action, and the quality of that assessment is directly tied to the diversity of perspectives informing it.**

Okay, one more story before we move onto Chapter 7. This one centers around one my favorite consumer archetypes: *hungry boyfriend.*

It was a Friday night in New York City, and in walked a young woman and her hungry boyfriend. She'd just received an email about a new delivery of fashion boots and was dying to get them before they sold out. Meanwhile, the hungry boyfriend was dying to eat. Our manager picked up on this as he complained to his girlfriend. He was worried that they wouldn't have time for dinner before their event now that they'd detoured into the store.

Our manager certainly didn't want the woman to feel rushed or stressed, but hungry boyfriend persisted. So she did what good managers in a belief-minded culture do: after she listened, she assessed his stated (vocal) and unstated (never asked us to do anything about it) need—hunger—and figured out a way to solve it.

At that point, every manager had iPads with the Seamless app attached to our store account. Without missing a beat, our manager handed the woman off to another associate and turned to hungry boyfriend.

"What would you like to eat?" she asked. He was shocked. Before he could even answer, she'd opened the app. Together they landed on burgers from a nearby restaurant. She even gave him a bottle of Corona, which we kept on hand for guests. He went off and sat on our couch, visibly relaxed.

Meanwhile, the girlfriend—obviously relieved—bought the boots along with two other items. The burgers came, hungry boyfriend thanked everyone, and the couple walked into the night carrying their bags. More than that, they both left transformed by an unexpected moment of thoughtfulness.

There I go again jumping ahead to transformation. Actually. I didn't jump ahead this time. See, our manager had actually led the couple through the entire CADET process in that one exchange:

- She **connected** through listening, and **assessed** with an eye toward solving.
- Then she literally **delivered** a beer and burgers for hungry boyfriend, plus a quiet shopping experience for the girlfriend.
- This completely **exceeded** everyone's expectation: the boyfriend didn't expect to be taken care of but was, the girlfriend didn't expect to get those boots before she was nagged to death (but she did), and the store made two additional sales on top of the boots.
- The couple's view of the Tory Burch brand was forever **trans-**

formed. What had started out as a potential point of friction became a moment of actual joy.

ASSESSMENT IS ONGOING

Like connection, assessment is not a one-time event but an ongoing cycle...a continuous loop of listening, learning, refining, and realigning.

Assessment sharpens our understanding, deepens our insight, and strengthens our ability to make decisions that truly deliver. When you weave assessment into the fabric of how you lead, it transforms how you solve problems, seize opportunities, and shape what comes next.

Much like the happy story of the hungry boyfriend, the thing that comes after assessment is delivery. We've touched upon it a few times already. Now let's take a closer look at what it means to deliver with purpose and impact.

> Assessment sharpens our understanding, deepens our insight, and strengthens our ability to make decisions that truly deliver.

Loyalty among employees and customers doesn't come from just one great experience. It comes from a sustained effort that involves delivering, refining, and delivering again.

CHAPTER 7

Deliver

DO AND DO AGAIN

Understanding starts when you connect. Clarity comes as you assess. Trust builds during both phases but doesn't become a meaningful currency until you deliver.

If connection and assessment set the groundwork, delivering is where everything comes to life. It shows your people that you're serious about acting on belief. It proves that you listened and acted on what you heard...that you walked the walk, not just talked the talk.

If connecting and assessing tell people you're on their side, then delivering *shows them* you are. It's a tangible demonstration of belief in action that can absolutely transform teams from compliant to committed. When you deliver, trust shoots into full bloom, and belief takes root to stay.

Leaders who understand this don't treat connecting, assessing, and delivering as three separate phases. They're not checking their calendars to figure out which day they should connect or when they should start assessing. These elements are always happening, often in tandem. They understand that connecting, assessing, and delivering are all part of the same ongoing cycle.

> ## If connecting and assessing tell people you're on their side, then delivering *shows them* you are.

They also understand that without delivering, all the other work will fall flat. They need to deliver. They also need their people to deliver in order to strengthen the bonds of trust and make future connections and assessments richer and sharper.

As an example, in my experience something that's worse than not asking for feedback is asking for it then doing nothing in response. Think about the hungry boyfriend from the last chapter. If our manager had simply ignored him, focused on the sale, and moved on, we would have had one outcome. Now imagine this version: she connects and assesses his situation, even *promises* burgers, then either changes her mind, drops the ball, or some combination. Now what's the outcome? How quickly would *hungry* become *hangry*? Is hungry boyfriend "happy she at least tried" or worse off because she gave him false hope. I'm glad we never had to find out.

It can be even worse when employees feel like you've manipulated or taken advantage of their time and insight...when the employee surveys lead to no action and become symbols of empty promises. Why tell employees that their voices matter if you're going to ignore their input? Misleading employees like this will only make a bad situation worse. Employee disengagement and disconnection can become disillusionment pretty quickly.

All this to say, delivery matters. Execution matters. Doing them both well and timely matters.

FROM DISCONNECTION TO BELIEF

When I was hired as COO of Bergdorf Goodman by the new president, we both walked into a culture that was challenged to say the least. Employees, many of them long term, were frustrated, disengaged, and angry about what had happened to their beloved brand. Any previous trust was long gone, and many employees had adopted an "us vs. them" mindset.

> **Delivery matters. Execution matters. Doing them both well and timely matters.**

The first thing I did was to meet with all eleven-hundred employees from across every department: stores, corporate, restaurant...everyone from everywhere. We met in groups of ten at a time so I could learn about the brand, its existing culture, opportunities, and challenges.

As listening tours go, it was a huge investment of time. Honestly, it was some of the best and most memorable time I spent during my entire tenure with the brand.

Connecting helped me learn and understand. Through those connections I gained clarity, which helped me see ways we could challenge existing paradigms as a group.

Many of the employees saw these meetings as the first chance they'd ever had to express their voices and have agency in regards to redirecting the ship. Someone was *finally* listening to them.

The meetings weren't easy. People had *a lot* of opinions, not to mention heaps of frustration. They also had some very positive intangibles, namely passion, a love of the brand, and a desire for it to be amazing again. Translation: they were frustrated because they cared.

I was able to complete about five sessions a week and took a few months to meet with every employee. Throughout the process, my goal was to make sure two things happened on the way to building trust: (1) I wanted to be transparent to the entire organization about these meetings and what I was learning, and (2) I wanted them to know it wasn't just lip service or a dog and pony show that wouldn't yield anything.

To hit this goal, I sent out a weekly company-wide email with the following subject line: "You said. We heard. We did." The email's purpose was simple: to reflect back what I'd learned that week (connecting), to share how it translated to needed action (assessing), and to highlight the actions we took (delivering). It's another example of something I shared with you earlier: this work does not have to be grandiose. In fact, what you'll find is sometimes the most basic responses and actions create the most profoundly positive reactions.

For instance, one week I learned that we had lights out on the selling floor and that it had been that way for months. I don't mean just a few lights. More than *two-hundred* lights were out! Why didn't anyone notice? Had people just gotten used to working in the dark?

Guess what we did. That's right: we changed lightbulbs. It took us two weeks to solve that situation, but we solved it. Again, on paper it was extremely simple. But things like belief and trust don't happen on paper. They happen in hearts. When people see you deliver on their feedback, it's a game-changer when it comes to repairing and rebuilding trust.

For Bergdorf at the time, it also helped rebuild pride in the brand that employees said they "used to" feel. Finally, it *showed* employees just how much their voices mattered. They recognized that they had agency, responsibility, and authority to make things better. By keeping and delivering on these and other promises, we began to turn our culture away from being compliance-minded and back to being committed.

> Things like belief and trust don't happen
> on paper. They happen in hearts.

TREATING EMPLOYEES LIKE ADULTS

Lots of organizations claim that their people are their greatest asset, but they don't always treat them that way. They micromanage decisions, restrict autonomy, and limit creative problem-solving. True delivery begins with treating employees like adults. This means trusting them to make smart decisions, supporting their growth, and giving them the freedom to execute on their insights. And respecting them enough to feel responsibility to deliver for them, every time.

Bad news happens. It's simply the nature of business, regardless of the type of business you're in. You're not always going to be breaking sales records. What I've found is that given the chance, people will rise to the level of trust you place in them and they have in you. When employees feel like they play an important role in finding the solution, they will deliver in ways that surprise even the most experienced leaders.

Of course there's a caveat here. If you haven't been connecting with your people from the jump, how can you suddenly expect them to get on your side or to rise up and give an extra effort for the sake of the brand? If you haven't delivered for them, why would they deliver for you? If they haven't seen their place on the path forward all along, why should they now?

A brand that consistently delivers doesn't just set high standards for their teams or try to whip people into shape. They steadily and regularly equip their people with the resources, autonomy, and support they need to meet the various standards and expectations they set.

Let me add a note here, since many of the examples I've shared come from the world of retail. The principles I'm trying to drive home transcend industries. In other words, when you treat employees like thoughtful, capable adults, engage them in the process of finding the way forward, deliver on your promises, and equip them with the knowledge, tools, resources, and freedom to deliver for each other and for customers, you create a culture of scalable, sustainable excellence.

So, whether we're talking about brands in financial services, tech, healthcare, or some other sector, the ones that consistently deliver at a high level for customers are the same ones that first deliver *for* their people. They create environments where employees are trusted to think, act, and solve problems with an owner's mindset. These organizations and their leaders provide clarity, not control, and support, not surveillance. In doing so, they cultivate cultures of accountability, creativity, and pride.

Simply put, when companies invest in delivering for their people, their people deliver for the business.

CLOSING THE GAP BETWEEN INTENT AND ACTIONS

One of the most common pitfalls I've seen get in the way of being able to deliver consistently lies in the disconnect between what leaders *say* they value and what actually happens on the ground. It's easy to say that employees come first, but do your policies, practices, and daily decisions reflect those words? Or is this yet another case where breakroom posters are full of sunshine and slogans, while the lived experience is anything but cheery?

Simply put, when companies invest in delivering for their people, their people deliver for the business.

Along these same lines, it's easy to *say* customer experience is a priority. However, unless employees have responsibility and authority to make real-time, customer-focused decisions, their stiffness or fear of breaking protocol will impact experiences for the worse.

On that note, excelling at delivering exceptional experiences takes more than just talking about values or patting employees on the back and telling them to "do their best." You have to build systems, then encourage your people to act on them. One of the most effective ways to do this is to eliminate barriers to action. Employees need to feel empowered to make decisions, take risks, and creatively solve problems without fearing backlash.

Creating this reality requires more than just verbal encouragement or cheerleading. Your employees need tools and authority to act on their instincts. If a front-line worker sees a way to improve a customer's experience—hungry boyfriend again—but lacks the ability to implement something, or doesn't feel like they have a channel where they can uplevel, the opportunity evaporates.

Employees need to feel empowered to make decisions, take risks, and creatively solve problems without fearing backlash.

When I was at Apple, I liked to hear from other organizations, in and outside retail, as a way to learn what their version of "the best" looked like in regards to employee-driven customer experiences. One story that still sticks with me took place at a Four Seasons in Scottsdale, Arizona.

As the story goes, a guest was checking out after a four-night stay. He was a frequent Four Seasons guest across their entire portfolio and also a business traveler. When the front desk employee asked the obvious question, "How was your stay?" His answer took her aback. "Awful," he muttered.

She followed up and asked why. He explained that for the last two nights the people in the casita next to his partied until dawn. He hadn't been able to sleep at all, and it wrecked his work days.

The employee was moved, committed, and motivated to make it right. Instead of asking why he didn't call the manager and pass him off to someone else, she decided to take full responsibility: she profusely apologized and decided to refund his entire stay. The traveler, who by now was completely floored at being seen and heard like this, accepted and left happy with an amazing turnaround story to share with others as well as renewed loyalty to Four Seasons.

That's not where the story ends. The Four Seasons had a process for logging such issues. Every morning the leadership team would do an after-action review of each complaint. When they read this one, they looked into what happened and realized there was a wedding party booked next to this guest. They decided to act in a major way, completely rezoning the property into two areas, one for business guests, the other for leisure.

They didn't stop there. They went a step further, reaching out to the employee who had made the on-the-spot decision to refund the guest and commending her for doing the right thing. While losing four nights of revenue wasn't ideal, their focus remained on the north star of customer loyalty. They were grateful she hadn't let a loyal guest walk away frustrated.

In fact, they used the moment as a learning opportunity, equipping her and other hosts with additional tools to handle similar situations in the future. Tools that could preserve both revenue *and* guest satisfaction.

The message was clear: she had made the right call, and now she had even more ways to do so moving forward.

MAKING EVERYTHING WORK

The effort you put in as a leader is the key to making any of this—and all of this—work for your employees and your customers. This goes all the way back to what I wrote at the start of the chapter: delivering should be baked in as part of your ongoing cadence, just the same as connecting and assessing.

Delivering must follow a deliberate and transparent rhythm, something I referenced earlier: *"You said. We heard. We did."* It's a powerful sequence, but only when a leader honors all three parts.

You can't stop at *"You said"* or *"We heard."* Well, you can, but if your goal is to create momentum, alignment, or trust, progress will stall if you don't actually deliver. You need to pair outputs with the inputs.

Meanwhile, skipping straight from *"You said"* to *"We did"* is just as problematic. It bypasses critical reflection and mutual understanding. Without that bridge, you risk misinterpreting the need and delivering something misaligned or ineffective.

Equally, *"We did"* on its own reflects a top-down approach. It signals action, yes, but not one rooted in connection or informed by context. True delivery must reflect the insights you gather during connection (*you said*) and assessment (*we heard*). That's how you earn not just compliance but commitment.

In a nutshell: delivering is the product of the work you put in *before* you deliver. It's also the sign that says you understand. If you want to deliver flawlessly, every time, make sure you follow the journey without thinking you can skip steps. It doesn't work that way.

As I've pointed out a few times already, none of this has to be about making grand gestures. Sure, if that's your style, then go for it—but it doesn't have to be.

More often than not, delivering is as simple as making sure people feel heard, acknowledged, and supported in their roles. It might involve pulling someone aside and letting them know how their feedback started a chain reaction, or sending a note that reads, "Remember when you mentioned this issue a few weeks ago? Well, we're doing these things to correct it. Thank you for bringing it to my attention."

CARRYING DELIVERY INTO THE WORLD

The best brand experiences don't come from rigid scripts or policies. They come from employees who feel empowered to go above and beyond. When employees feel supported, they don't just deliver internally. They take this energy into customer interactions.

The equation on this isn't rocket science. When employees experience excellence *internally*, they pass it on *externally*. Even better, customers can tell when employees believe in what they're doing. Even better than that: these same customers want to be part of what's happening. They'll look for ways to support your brand.

The best brand experiences don't come from rigid scripts or policies. They come from employees who feel empowered to go above and beyond.

Working from this perspective reinforces something I keep banging on about: delivery is not a one-and-done task. Here's an example. Your employees complain about the lighting in the breakroom constantly being out. No one wants to go in there at all. Solution: you change the lightbulbs. Are you done? Of course not. Instead, you've set the stage for an ongoing effort. What else can change around the workplace?

Guess what happens when you make connecting a key part of your leadership style? You gain trust by being available. Later, when your organization needs to figure out a way to train up employees, you go to them to find out what will work. You gather intel, which is easy because you already have rapport. Then you and a group of employees devise a plan. You present it, gain buy-in, and roll it out. Conversation, conversion, delivery, execution. Again and again.

This is the cycle winning brands understand and follow. They don't just rush to solve problems; they embed the notion of delivering into their culture.

That's it, right? Not quite.

When I use the word *cycle*, I'm referring to the process, not the specific thing being delivered. That "thing" is always changing. One day it's lightbulbs, the next it's training, communication, or PTO. The subject will shift. The process shouldn't.

> **Winning brands understand and follow this cycle. They don't just rush to solve problems; they embed the notion of delivering into their culture.**

What remains constant is the rhythm of connecting, assessing, and delivering, as well as the ongoing refinement of how well you're doing each step. This isn't a one-time pass. It's a practice:

- Make it easy for employees to regularly share what's working, what's not, and where friction is building.
- Establish real feedback loops. I'm not just talking about surveys here but systems for listening and acting.
- Define and uphold delivery nonnegotiables. Set the bar, and hold yourself and others accountable to it.
- Use data and metrics to *start* the conversation, not end it. Insight comes from understanding the inputs that drive the outputs.
- Commit to a learning culture. When you see every experience, be it good, bad, or in between, as valuable, you build the foundation for more effective, more human delivery.

Ultimately, delivering is about taking action. It's where insights, strategies, and connections materialize into real, tangible outcomes. It's what turns words into impacts and intentions from transformation.

A few final thoughts on delivering:

- Even when flawless execution is your north star, don't let the idea of perfection hold you back from actually doing. Here's another saying most of us have heard: "Great is the enemy of good." To deliver at all, you have to deliver *the first time*, even if it's not perfect. If you have a learning culture in place, then delivery can be something that you refine and perfect, but not delivering is not an option.
- Delivering is also about consistency, which builds trust. It's about showing up, following through, and being willing to adapt when things don't go as planned, again and again and again. It's about believing and embodying the following statement: "I can count on you, and you can count on me."
- Leaders and brands must recognize that execution isn't a moment but a mindset. To get to that point, you have to create an environment where people are empowered, trusted, and equipped to bring their best selves to their roles. That requires understanding that delivery is more than a phase. It's the literal heartbeat of a thriving brand.

Of everything I've written in the last three chapters, as we've covered connecting, assessing, and delivering, I want to leave you with one of my most essential beliefs: loyalty among employees and customers doesn't come from just one great experience. It comes from a sustained effort that involves delivering, refining, and delivering again. It's about proving, but it's also about improving. That's how brands make and keep promises.

So is this the end of the road? Flawless execution and consistent delivering? Absolutely not. Now is where the fun begins—now you get to think about all the ways to exceed expectations. To step into the emotional space of unstated needs.

Let's move in that direction next as we head into Part 3.

Part 3

Between delivering and exceeding exists a true divide, something I call the chasm of satisfaction. Crossing the chasm is the difference between meeting expectations and forging enduring loyalty.

CHAPTER 8

Exceed

MAKE THE LEAP

Brands that thrive don't just execute well or deliver on promises and walk away. They constantly ask, "What else can we do?" They go beyond functional and into the aspirational, truly creating moments that matter. This is what exceeding is all about.

When I created the framework at the core of this book, I recognized that this work tends to unfold in two phases. The first phase includes the stages I discussed in Part 2. Part 3 takes us deeper into the realm of exceeding and eventually transforming.

Many brands, once they reach the delivering phase, stay put, content to fulfill promises without pressing further. Why not? Delivering on what's promised is no small feat. However, here's a critical point at the heart of this chapter: between delivering and exceeding exists a true divide, something I call the *chasm of satisfaction*.

Crossing the chasm is the difference between meeting expectations and forging enduring loyalty. Can you make the leap?

DELIVERING IS NOT THE END

When you deliver flawlessly, you satisfy a stated need, whether for an employee or a customer. That's great, but it isn't where you should stop. To deliver is to say, "I have heard your stated needs, and I have met them." Exceeding, on the other hand, happens when you focus on the *unstated* needs, the small but powerful extras that show people how much you value them.

Exceeding happens in those moments when you go beyond what's functional and start to move toward what's aspirational, with an eye on developing new opportunities in the future. This is the way you create loyalty, which is the gift someone gives you because you've become relevant to them on a whole new level.

THE SATISFACTION TRAP

Years ago, a lot of companies jumped into the idea of running satisfaction surveys. That's exactly what they wanted to learn from people: "Are you satisfied?" Here's what they found: even when 70 percent of people said they *were* satisfied with a product, service, or experience, they were still willing to jump ship to another brand or a better experience.

> Exceeding happens in those moments when you go beyond what's functional and start to move towards what's aspirational, with an eye on developing new opportunities in the future.

Satisfaction alone does not create loyalty. If loyalty is a true currency, then what does it actually mean for brands?

For starters, loyalty aligns with a person's willingness to

recommend a brand or an experience to friends, colleagues, coworkers, and the like. It also aligns with their willingness to do so on their own, with no need for a coupon or some kind of recognition. Today we refer to this as being a brand "evangelist" or "advocate."

Gaining this insight has been a boon for brands that can answer the next question: "How do we actually create loyalty?"

Just to be clear, I'm not talking about loyalty programs but true brand loyalty. Loyalty programs are promotional tools or vehicles for discounts and incentives that help drive purchases by reducing costs. Most brands have some kind of loyalty program, which are fine as sales tools. But a loyalty program is not the loyalty I'm talking about.

Brand loyalty is much different and much bigger. It's a gift that customers give freely to the brand. People commit because they care, not because the brand is buying their commitment with off-the-shelf perks. Brands earn this gift through creating meaning and relevance and steadily adding value to people's lives.

> **Brand loyalty is much different and much bigger. It's a gift that customers give freely to the brand.**

Let's recap the satisfaction trap before we go forward:

- If your brand is effectively connecting, assessing, and delivering, you're halfway there.
- Be careful if you think just delivering will create sustainable momentum. In reality, employees, customers, or both will eventually signal that it won't.

- Delivering may earn satisfaction, but if your goal is to cultivate lasting loyalty both inside and outside the organization, you need to focus on exceeding.

PROVING AND IMPROVING

Here's one of my most essential beliefs: creating loyalty among employees and customers doesn't happen because of one great experience. It comes from a sustained effort that starts when you deliver, then builds with the moments of exceeding. In that way, you have to keep proving yourself. You also have to keep *learning and refining understanding* in order to know how to exceed. That's how a brand both makes and keeps promises.

The big idea behind *exceeding* leads to deeper, essential questions every brand should be willing to ask itself: "What more can we do for you?" "How can we become more relevant to your life?" "How do we create an authentic emotional connection?"

Remember, exceeding isn't just about meeting stated needs. It's about going beyond them. It's also about listening for meaning, constantly tuning into the unspoken, subtle signals that lie between the lines of what someone is saying or requesting (or not saying, not requesting).

When you exceed, it's a sign that you're anticipating, sensing, and delivering what people didn't even think to ask for or perhaps didn't realize they wanted or needed. The hungry boyfriend from Chapter 6 didn't ask us to order him burgers or give him a beer. He simply stated he was hungry.

People aren't static. Neither are relationships. Growth, learning, and refinement are all about staying relevant to who someone is *now*, not who they were.

Here's a simple example of how ongoing connection and thoughtful assessment empower a brand to exceed expectations.

Imagine a company relying on data from three years ago...back when I *might have been* motivated by discounts. Today, what excites me is early access to new products. If the brand still sees me through that outdated lens, they'll send me another coupon and completely miss the chance to invite me to a private preview of their new collection. Actually, they won't just miss the mark on delivery. They'll also lose the opportunity to truly exceed.

My point: people are dynamic. Relationships between people and brands are like those between neighbors, friends, siblings: either growing or dying. If you aren't investing in true, deep, meaningful understanding, then using that to find ways to go beyond the baseline, people will fade away. For brands, those people are internal and external customers.

SMALL GESTURES, BIG IMPACTS

Stop me if you've read this already, but this work doesn't require grand, sweeping gestures. I know, right. I'm a broken record. Don't worry. I'm doing it on purpose. I had a boss who used to say, "Repetition doesn't spoil the prayer." She was right. So let me repeat: it's true that the smallest, most thoughtful actions can create the biggest impact.

> If you aren't investing in true, deep, meaningful understanding, then using that to find ways to go beyond the baseline, people will fade away.

Here's a perfect example from a conversation I had with the chairman of a prominent private equity firm. He and I were seated next to each other at a dinner, and he asked about my strategy at Bergdorf Goodman. I explained that after spending time getting to understand our customer, one truth became clear: while people of means can purchase mostly whatever they want, what remains rare—what money *cannot* buy—is thoughtfulness. Our focus would not simply be on meeting stated needs but on anticipating and exceeding the unspoken ones. We would create moments of joy.

He listened, paused, then told me a story about a bookmark.

His favorite hotel was the George V in Paris. He was also an avid reader. Those details both matter in the context of the story. One evening, after checking in, he had a few moments before dinner. He took out his book and started to read. When he realized he was running late, he grabbed a crumpled scrap of paper from his bag, tucked it sticking out between the pages, closed the book, and set it on the nightstand.

Later when he returned to his room, he saw that the staff had performed their usual turndown service. They'd also done something unexpected: replaced the torn piece of paper with a beautiful bookmark.

He was so moved by the gesture that he still had the bookmark more than five years later. He could have bought ten thousand bookmarks. He probably could have bought a bookmark-making business if he'd wanted to. But the bookmark reminded him of that single act of thoughtfulness—that fleeting, unexpected moment of joy. That's what stayed with him.

He hadn't asked for a bookmark. The simple act told him that someone had taken extra time, effort, and consideration to do something beyond their job description. Whoever it was had seen something they could make better, and they took the chance. They cared about doing it. It may have been a light touch in the grand scheme of life, but it was poignant all the same.

Here's how this particular equation breaks down. First, the hotel's staff had delivered the expectation: they turned the linens, changed the towels, and freshened up the room. Then they exceeded with something small that went above and beyond and created a lasting effect.

Now let's replay it a little differently. Imagine that the chairman returned to his room and saw that the bed was still a mess and the wet towels were on the bathroom floor where he'd left them, but he had a brand new bookmark. Would this still be exceeding?

Even if the cleaning staff saw it as exceeding, the chairman probably would have been disappointed. Actually, he probably would have been troubled by the fact that they came into his room, changed his bookmark, and left everything else the same. I know I would have been.

Exceeding or not, the act would have been a failure because they wouldn't have executed on the delivery. If they'd skipped the delivery piece, how could the chairman have even paid attention to the exceeding piece? He would have been too distracted by the fact that his room was still a mess.

The bottom line: when delivery goes wrong, people don't notice the extras. They notice what's missing.

At the core of this understanding is something I've been writing since the start of the book: the stages of this framework are interconnected and build on one another in a natural, intentional flow. You simply can't *exceed* expectations without first delivering on your core promise. You must meet a person's stated need before you earn the right to move past the space of satisfaction and get to loyalty and transformation.

When delivery goes wrong, people don't notice the extras. They notice what's missing.

It's a progressive journey, and there are no shortcuts. It's sort of like the old GINSU Knife commercials from the late '80s. If you're not familiar, look them up on YouTube. They're pretty entertaining. They always had the same refrain: "But wait, there's more!"

For a brand that cares about exceeding, this translates to "We'll start by meeting your expectations, then we'll look for ways to add even more value."

THE LISTENING LINK

This is a good time to revisit hungry boyfriend from Chapter 6. You remember him, I'm sure. His girlfriend was on the hunt for boots in Tory Burch's New York City store. He was...well... he was hungry. You already know the ending: we took care of both of them.

I'm coming back to this story because it highlights the way our manager was really listening and truly tuning in. When hungry boyfriend groaned, "But I'm hungry," she didn't ignore it. She heard him, which sparked a chain of thinking. First, *what can we do?* And then, *let's handle it.*

One big part of the story I want to drive home relates to the fact that our store manager not only heard his unstated need, but she also understood his girlfriend's stated and unstated needs. She *really* needed those boots, which we knew right away. She was literally holding her phone up to show us the email she'd received.

What was the unstated need? Simply put, she needed a little

space from hungry boyfriend so she could enjoy her shopping experience. In that way, giving the hungry boyfriend a beer and a bag of burgers was as much about the girlfriend as anything else. She was already moving as quickly as she could. He was only making her feel more rushed. She wanted the process to be as easy and pleasant as possible.

In the end, taking care of both of them separately was a big part of exceeding. But again, it all started with listening.

WHAT PREVENTS EXCEEDING?

What holds brands back from exceeding? Is it complacency? Compliance? A lack of understanding how humans develop loyalty?

Let's say a brand consistently delivers but never pushes beyond that. Maybe that's intentional. Maybe they're aiming for basic, functional satisfaction. The kind where customers say, "I got exactly what I asked for. That's fine." Or maybe leadership sets the bar just high enough, figures "People seem happy," and stops there.

It happens all the time. In fact, it's happening right now. We've all walked away from brands that stopped feeling meaningful and where the emotional connection just faded.

Yes, I'm talking about *emotion* here. That's because emotional investment is the fuel that drives the momentum of exceeding. It's a subtle, powerful tug, the feeling of knowing that someone went out of their way to hear, see, and serve you. It's personal. It's the bookmark you didn't ask for and weren't expecting. It says, "We hear you. We get you."

Here's a fast personal anecdote. A few weeks ago, I was on a flight that got delayed. For five hours, I sat in the terminal watching the departure time slide back in thirty-minute increments. Eventually, the flight was canceled and pushed to the next day. Everyone on the canceled flight and I came back in the morning—only to find another delay.

Emotional investment is the fuel that drives the momentum of exceeding.

When we finally boarded, the flight attendants did their best to make the experience as positive as possible. They were kind, upbeat, and apologetic. But the damage was done. No amount of vouchers or drink coupons could fix our bad moods or the sour taste we all shared for this particular airline. The poor staff members were just trying to exceed, but since the airline hadn't delivered, it was moot. They were basically throwing good money after bad. All any of us wanted was to get to our next destination, and we were already a day behind schedule.

That's a customer-facing example. What about employees? What happens when a brand taps out at good enough? What does it say to the people on the inside when a brand never aspires to exceed? That's where the emotional disconnection starts. Once it does, the momentum doesn't just stall. It starts to roll backward.

THE GULF BETWEEN DELIVERING AND EXCEEDING

Remember the *chasm of satisfaction* from the start of the chapter? Now I'd like to introduce you to the gulf between delivering and exceeding the expectations of internal customers.

It's important to remember a few dynamics at play when it comes to exceeding (or failing to exceed) for employees. First, let's acknowledge a hard truth: in many workplace cultures, there's a lingering mindset that says employees are simply a means to an end. If you've ever found yourself on the receiving end of that thinking, I'm genuinely sorry. If you're in a position to shift that mindset, I hope this book helps you see the real value in doing so.

To be fair, there are also companies that understand the impact of their decisions and are actively trying to strengthen and/or repair their connections with people. Still, even with the best intentions, their efforts can come off as hollow. Why? Often it's because they're skipping steps, trying to leap from *connecting* straight to *exceeding*. It can feel pretty inauthentic when that happens. Are they trying to gloss over a deeper issue? Appease discontent? Compensate for being late to the game?

Brands need to keep in mind that the relationships they have with employees are human relationships. A brand cannot treat people as transactional and then suddenly hope to pivot toward talking about visions, shared purposes, and north stars. That type of abrupt shift doesn't inspire trust. It just feels like a cop-out.

One very basic example that comes up time and time again in the world of retail is the concept of "consistent hours." When you're an hourly employee working in retail, one of the last things you want is to be on the unforgiving yo-yo of inconsistency. Ten hours this week, twenty-five the next, twelve hours the week after that. This type of scheduling might make sense for managers, but not for employees. In fact, this reinforces the negative stereotype I mentioned above: that employees are just a means to an end.

A brand cannot treat people as transactional and then suddenly hope to pivot toward talking about visions, shared purposes, and north stars.

You want to know how to make a tough situation even worse? Try throwing a pizza party for a team that's already frustrated or checked out.

When I jokingly mentioned a pizza party back in Chapter 6, it wasn't just a throwaway line. Seriously, nothing screams *"We're not listening"* like tossing slices of lukewarm pizza at people who are asking for something real. We've all been to those parties. I definitely have. And I've heard the same thing more times than I can count: *"I wish they'd spend this money on giving me more hours than on cheese and crust."*

This highlights a much deeper issue: tone-deafness. When employees are asking for the basics—things like stability, support, fair treatment, opportunities—yet the response is a pizza party, that's not exceeding. That's insulting.

Instead of sending the message "You spoke, we listened, we acted," it ends up sounding more like "You spoke, we understood...but we aren't going to give you what you really need, so please accept this and move on."

I remember when I was at Gap, senior leadership would occasionally grow frustrated with how stores were delivering on standards, merchandising, or service. The field leadership, while fully aligned with the vision and the expectations, would explain that the resources allocated by finance weren't sufficient to execute on the vision. The usual response? Bring in an outside firm to conduct a "time and motion study," essentially a detailed breakdown of every task, tracking how long it took to do things right.

The findings were always the same: the true cost of meeting expectations was far greater than the resources stores were given.

And every time, the response was identical: put the report in a drawer, lock it, and pretend it didn't exist. Expectations stayed the same. Resources didn't budge. And frontline teams were left with the impossible job of doing more with less. They were unable to deliver, let alone exceed.

Here's the truth: exceeding doesn't happen by accident. Brands need clarity around expectations, alignment across teams, and meaningful investment to support the work. Without that, it's just noise masquerading as strategy.

YOUR GOODWILL ACCOUNT

On the opposite side of the spectrum is something I refer to as having a *goodwill account*. There are many ways brands and leaders can invest or deposit into their respective goodwill accounts.

> **Exceeding doesn't happen by accident. Brands need clarity around expectations, alignment across teams, and meaningful investment to support the work.**

The easiest way to build a goodwill account: to meet stated needs, deliver on promises, and keep your ears open for the unstated needs to exceed expectations. What are some ways this might show up in a brand? Not to keep ringing the same bell...but they're simple. Here are a few:

- You treat people with respect and dignity.
- You promise and deliver a good wage and benefits.
- You offer training and professional enrichment opportunities.
- You help employees see that this is a path toward a career, not just a job.

Yes, these types of actions say that you care about delivering on your employees' expectations. When you meet them, you're saying that you see them as your greatest asset and as partners in the business—not as means to an end. Better yet, you'll add to your goodwill account.

Now, your goodwill account is kind of like a bank account. There are times when you make deposits via trust, consistency, and care. And there are also times when you make withdrawals, sometimes unintentionally.

No brand or leader *wants* to deplete their goodwill, but many do. Here are a few common (and avoidable) ways brands end up making those withdrawals:

- You overpromise and underdeliver.
- You speak *for* employees but not *with* them.
- You issue top-down directives from a distant "ivory tower."
- You ask for feedback but then disregard it (which is worse than not asking at all).

What's the best way to build your goodwill account as a leader? For me, it starts with treating employees like adults, which includes respecting them as people, giving them agency, and offering them a real voice in shaping the brand. That can look different depending on your company's reality. Maybe it's a simple, consistent practice like sharing a "You said, we heard, we did" update. Maybe it's more.

Sometimes it means pulling people together to talk through the hard stuff, not just the wins. If hours are being cut, explain why. Even more importantly, what if you let employees in on the *why* before they had to ask? Trust is built in moments like these. Not with perfection but with honesty, inclusion, and respect.

KEEPING PROMISES

You've probably heard the saying, "The road to hell is paved with good intentions." I bring it up here because one of the quickest ways a company can burn through goodwill is by making promises it doesn't keep.

Lots of brands *mean* well. They're out there trying to create a better experience for employees, customers, even the communities they serve. No matter how noble the intent, failing to follow through on a promise is one of the most damaging missteps any brand can make.

This goes beyond not delivering on the basics. You always need to meet core expectations. But if you're going to step into the space of *exceeding*...if you're going to say, "We're ready to do more," then you *have* to follow through. If you can't, don't make the promise.

It's easy for leaders to get swept up in the desire to inspire. They'll make grand proclamations about what they are going to do, how things are going to change, get better, etc. Maybe they genuinely mean it. Sadly, when those promises don't materialize, first they fade, then they leave a gaping hole.

From an employee's perspective, here's what that looks like:

the first time a promise falls flat, it stings. It feels like someone has pulled the rug out from under you. If it happens again, the initial sting turns into skepticism.

Eventually, employees stop hoping and start rolling their eyes. Some may speak up. Others will just quietly disengage. In time, they might even start their own version of internal messaging that sounds something like: "They asked, we answered, they ignored us."

It might not sound like the most exciting approach to building trust with employees, but I've always believed in the power of being realistic to the point of quietly overdelivering when possible. In my experience, employees don't want smoke and mirrors or grand gestures that come at the cost of real follow-through.

Something that inspires people is consistency. It's showing up, doing what you say you'll do, and being honest, even when the message isn't wrapped in fanfare. People have a remarkable ability to sense inauthenticity.

To put it plainly, they can spot the spin a mile away. So, what's the best way to keep making deposits in the goodwill account? Simple: don't let your heart make promises your head and hands can't keep.

THE REALITY OF EXCEEDING

Every brand evolves. Highs, lows, and plateaus are part of the journey. But where I've consistently seen brands *truly* exceed is when there's strong alignment between their culture and values, and those of its employees. That's when everything becomes a value-driven investment—where people do more than just speak beliefs but actually live them.

In these environments, things reach a point where leaders begin saying, "If I believe that development is important for our employees and that we want them to actually have careers here, then I have to put that belief to work. I'm going to invest in development programs. Not just that, but I'm going to loop them into the process. They'll help inform the direction we take." It becomes a financial manifestation of belief. Ideas become real. Actions occur beyond the words themselves. Delivery becomes a given, and exceeding becomes the new reality.

This approach isn't reserved for the good times only. Even during hard moments when we've had to make difficult decisions around hours, layoffs, or restructuring, I've brought the people most affected into the process. We created options, then asked employees which felt most fair, equitable, and manageable. And while some might assume this would invite chaos, the opposite happened. When people are respected enough to be included—and given agency—they shift from resistance to collaboration. They help solve the problem.

Trust me when I say this does not happen by accident. Nor is it magic. Actually, exceeding is the result of following some very basic tenets and tactics, starting with our old friend connecting.

Yes, we've almost come full circle because that's how progress works. You connect so people know you're listening. You assess by actually using what you've heard. And you deliver by taking thoughtful, informed action. Depending on the culture, this rhythm is what unlocks the path to exceeding.

I know I keep hitting this note, but it matters: the simple act of "you said, we heard, we did" can shift an entire culture, especially if that culture has been stuck in the fog of empty promises and inaction.

When you lead with your own version of "you said, we heard, we did," here's what people will actually think:

- My voice matters here.

- They're truly listening to me.
- They're translating what they heard into real steps.
- And they're inviting all of us to take those steps *together*.
- We'll even help connect the dots as we go so nothing gets lost in translation.

This is more than a proof-point. This is engagement. And it's extremely functional. On the front-end, it's all about inviting, listening, and acting. As time goes on, it opens up the path that leads toward exceeding and ideally transforming a culture where everyone is part of the mix, working toward loftier expectations again and again.

It's also another form of codification, specifically the codification of beliefs. When you enter into the space where a brand's beliefs align with what your people believe, something powerful emerges. The entire team exceeds. The collective mindset becomes "I can't believe I get to work here. Everything I care about lives in this place. I bleed this brand. I'm grateful. And I want to give something back."

That's what exceeding looks like when it becomes fully embedded. It's not a tactic. It's a culture.

Gap in the early '90s was the epitome of this type of strong, employee-first culture. It was more than just a great place to work. It was a place people didn't ever want to leave. Recruiters struggled trying to lure anyone away. Inside the company, we called it "bleeding blue."

Anyone who was there during that time knows exactly what that meant. It really was something special. Personally and professionally, I've never felt more supported as an employee, leader, or a person than I did at Gap. The investment the company made in me was real, and it left a lasting impact. I grew so much during my time there, and in return, I gave back what they gave me: commitment, loyalty, and a deep belief in the brand.

The role of a leader in the space of exceeding is to nurture and support people's natural human desire to go beyond—to grow, contribute, and thrive. If you've been fortunate, you've experienced environments like this as well. And if you've been *really* fortunate, you've helped create them. If that's true, then you already have a sense of what real transformation feels like.

> **The role of a leader in the space of exceeding is to nurture and support people's natural human desire to go beyond—to grow, contribute, and thrive.**

Whether the next chapter serves as a refresher or brand new information for you, now's the time to dive in and explore what transformation truly looks like.

Transformation is not a destination or an endpoint. It is a moment, a milestone, and a place where people can see, measure, feel, and experience real change.

CHAPTER 9

Transform

CHANGE FOR THE BETTER

To transform is to change: to become something new beyond what once was. Transformation is not just about change for its own sake; it's about meaningful impact, lasting outcomes, and the continuous evolution your brand undertakes collectively.

What does it mean to transform? Better yet, what does a leader have to do to help make it happen? Let's glance backward in order to answer that.

Before you can transform, you have to exceed. That's what our last chapter was all about. In order to exceed, you have to invest in making the leap across what I referred to as "the chasm of satisfaction." This means getting beyond the act of delivering.

When viewed through this lens, a leader's role in transformation comes down to cultivating an environment where people feel genuinely supported in their desire to grow, evolve, and become better versions of themselves.

INPUTS AND OUTPUTS

Almost every piece of a brand's journey is about the investments you make over time. This includes the energy, resources, and authentic care you put into connecting with people, assessing what you hear, delivering on promises, and exceeding beyond expectations.

Your investments should continue to align toward the goal of creating an environment where people at all levels understand what's at stake and know exactly how to operate within a framework they've helped to create. This drives transformation.

Transformation is not a destination or a static end point. It is a moment, a milestone, and a place where people can see, measure, feel, and experience real change. It is the culmination of all the inputs that have come before to create a new reality. It also becomes the starting point for next-level connection.

Once again, this journey isn't a straight line but a circle where each phase borrows something from the phase before it and feeds something into the next. In that way, the journey to ultimate transformation never ends, a fact that's both daunting and liberating when you really crack into it.

CREATING CONFIDENCE

The power of transformation into confidence lies in its ability to turn uncertainty into agency.

When someone transforms into confidence, they stop seeking permission and start stepping into possibility. They don't just take up space. They own it. And that shift changes how they lead, how they connect, and how they shape the world around them.

Confidence doesn't appear out of thin air. A leader has to cultivate it through clarity, support, and meaningful growth. Leaders rarely have the luxury of working only with seasoned professionals or senior executives. That's a good thing. Every stage of growth is an opportunity to develop emerging talent and guide individuals as they gain both competence and self-awareness.

When someone transforms into confidence, they stop seeking permission and start stepping into possibility.

While you can't force growth or rush evolution, you can absolutely create the conditions that accelerate it. One of the most powerful ways to do that? Front-load your time and attention.

Because here's the truth: **competence breeds confidence**.

If you want people to feel secure in their decisions, approaches, and professional judgment, you must equip them with tools, information, education, resources, and opportunities to practice sound decision-making. The sooner you begin, the more empowered they become.

Unfortunately, some leaders withhold these resources, consciously or otherwise. They guard information, limit access, and decide others aren't "ready" yet. Sometimes it's ego. Sometimes it's just legacy thinking wrapped in tradition: *"This is how we've always done it."*

But let's call that what it is: a culture of compliance, not empowerment.

No matter what's behind this type of thinking, the result will always be the same. When someone hoards power, transformation stalls. You don't create confident, capable decision-makers. You get cautious rule-followers waiting for permission.

And that's the difference. Empowered cultures create confident leaders. Controlled cultures create quiet ones. If you want transformation to happen, start by letting people grow into it. Then get out of their way.

> When someone hoards power,
> transformation stalls.

IN SERVICE OF SOMETHING BIGGER

Back in Chapter 4, I shared the story about my boss who explained what my career goal should be. In effect, he said I should aspire to "do nothing." His name was Fred Maas, and he was a genius in his own way. His words of wisdom still live with me.

Remember, I was just a buyer-in-training at the time. Part of my development involved a rotation in stores as a sales manager. It was my first experience managing people, and I was nervous. That's what prompted me to ask Fred for his guidance, which prompted him to say the magic words: "Your job is ultimately to do nothing."

Yes, it sounded great. When I think about it all these years later, it still makes me smile. His simple words held so much wisdom. Of course, Fred meant something different than what my twenty-two-year-old brain was translating.

What he was really saying was this: in order for me to "do nothing," everyone on my team needs to be capable of doing their job and mine.

Therefore, my *real* job was to develop the people around me so effectively that I could remove myself from aspects of the day-to-day, take on bigger challenges, and contribute to the company in more meaningful ways. Fred's wisdom reshaped the way I thought about leadership at every turn. It wasn't about being in control. It was about making myself unnecessary.

This mindset becomes even more important when you're leading through transformation. That's because transformation isn't about titles or job descriptions. It's about how leaders show up. This is especially true when cross-functional teams are involved: merchandising talking to operations, operations talking to finance, etc.

In these environments, you realize quickly that everyone is speaking a different language. They have different pain points and goals. Their incentives may even compete. It can be extremely complex, which is one of the main reasons why self-managed teams don't emerge naturally.

Without guidance, people often look to you, the leader, as the final translator, mediator, and equalizer. It's flattering to be needed, but the true goal is to build a team that doesn't need you in the center.

Let me return to something I mentioned in Chapter 4: **empowerment doesn't mean abandonment**.

If you want to lead with this mindset while still preparing people to thrive without you, it helps to view leadership as an act of service. That means walking alongside people as they grow, not just stepping aside and hoping they'll figure it out.

When I was leading the brand reinvention at Gap, one of our core goals was to shift store managers from being shopkeepers to becoming true business owners. For years, the company had operated under a top-down, command-and-control model. We were trying to change that and were inviting managers into a more collaborative, engaged way of leading while encouraging them to do the same with their teams.

To support this, we hosted weekly "summits" to teach new

concepts and introduce new ways of thinking. Then, managers would return to their stores and put those ideas into practice.

But one week, we started getting a wave of complaints from frontline employees. One story in particular stood out. A long-time team member brought out a shipment of new denim and asked his manager, "What would you like me to do with it?" It was a routine question in the old model. The manager, trying to apply the new approach, responded with, "I don't know. What do you think?"

The employee was confused, not to mention frustrated. No one had ever asked for his input before. There had been no context, no prep, and no gradual shift in expectations. The manager thought she was empowering him. From the employee's perspective, his manager was actually abandoning him.

Here's the truth: transformation isn't a sharp left turn but a journey you take together.

Empowerment requires intention, support, and shared understanding. Without those things, change can feel disorienting rather than inspiring. And that's when people pull back instead of stepping up.

However, when employees understand what they are solving for as a team, have agency, possess clarity about their roles, and begin to prioritize the collective over their individual departments, something powerful happens. They shift from defending their silos to aligning around a shared purpose. That's when real transformation begins.

Transformation isn't a sharp left turn but a journey you take together.

This shift doesn't happen on its own. If you want to build a self-directed team, you have to prioritize the idea of creating clarity and focus and continuing to foster and deepen relationships. You have to keep asking the questions in order to transform:

- "What are we solving for as a team?"
- "What does the team need to succeed?"
- "What is your role in making the team successful?"
- "How will we work together for the greater good of the team?"
- "What will get in our way of making this a reality?"

In my experience, when people embrace the idea of being in service to the team, they often discover that it's the smartest and most effective way to support themselves and their own groups... which brings me back around to Fred Maas's advice, which was both deceptively simple and profoundly true.

CREATING A SELF-DIRECTED TEAM

Years ago, I was leading a high-performing team of thirteen direct reports. They were senior leaders from different functions across the brand, including merchandising, planning, operations, store design, visual, training, operations—you name it. They led vastly different departments and had their own goals, agendas, and needs.

In a typical situation, a group like this would need someone above them to connect dots since they didn't do the same things. That was the position I was in. I wanted to change that. Did they *really* need me around to create alignment? Was my presence necessary in order to smoothen out debates or issues among them? I didn't think so.

My goal was for them to go from being a working group to being a self-directed, high-performing team. I wanted to take myself out of the equation and let them run their own meetings about business strategy without me. It would be a transformative initiative. How?

I didn't make a plan for this to happen on my own. Instead, *we* made a plan as a group. To get each of them involved in this process, I started where everything starts: connecting.

I made sure that they all understood the benefits of a self-directed team, how it would drive the business and develop each of them and all of them. After creating clarity and alignment, we embarked on a number of team-building offsites and strategy sessions to put things into place. From there, we assessed where we were and uncovered what they wanted and needed from the experience (the delivery piece). Then we designed a roadmap that essentially said, "This is how things will go once Matt steps away."

We continued to press forward without a firm date for when I'd step away. Then one day, ahead of our next meeting, the heads of planning and merchandising came into my office. They sat down, went through the usual pleasantries, then said, "Well, we're ready."

"For what?" I asked.

"We don't want you to be at the next meeting."

Talk about a strange moment. It's probably similar to watching your child pedal away a few seconds after you take off the training wheels. I felt a swell of pride, followed by an unexpected dose of fear.

"Oh," I said.

"Yeah," they went on. "We want to go through things as a group...without you. We want to come up with solutions, propose them, and then bring them to you to get your thoughts... approval, pushback, questions, whatever it might be."

"Sounds like a plan," I said, not letting on that the whole thing felt like I was being kicked out of the cool kids club. Still, this was the idea all along: embark on a mission toward creating a self-directed team.

They'd reached the moment where they were ready to take on the responsibility without me being there to manage the process. They knew what they had to do to guide themselves, find clarity, and support one another whenever they had to remove obstacles.

It was an incredibly rewarding time in my career, not just with them but across the entire spectrum of my professional life. Everyone on the team of thirteen had different functions, agendas, budgets, goals, and even occasional turf wars. It was a harder push with a more rewarding outcome because they truly embraced the idea of being in service to each other, rather than focusing exclusively on their own slice of pie.

The best part was the way this transformative success manifested among them. They saw how much they needed each other to succeed and benefited from one other's growth. Silos? Forget those. Fiefdoms? None at all.

As for me, it did free me up to focus on other ways to drive business differently. I had new opportunities to iterate on new ideas and thoughts or explore the brand through different lenses by reaching more people.

THE *WE* FACTOR OF TRANSFORMATION

It's important for every leader in a committed brand to move away from the idea that "I" know the answers or "I" will do the choosing. Whenever I've built a team or worked with an existing team, I've aimed to inspire their own sense of autonomy, responsibility, and authority.

I've gone to great lengths to make them part of the process

and never create anything in a vacuum. I've always focused on the idea that *we* create strategy, *we* identify opportunities and gaps, and so forth. Then *we* build solutions together. Oh...and *we* hold each other accountable for results. The best part is that in most cases, the solutions have indeed come from the input of team members.

It's important for every leader in a committed brand to move away from the idea that "I know the answers" or "I will do the choosing."

When people remain entrenched in a fiefdom mindset, the greatest driver in my opinion tends to be the structure of incentives that a company already has in place. Many companies talk about *working for the good of the brand*. Too often, though, those words add up to being a batch of lip service.

Here's the truth: when each department is measured against isolated, unaligned goals, the company is operating from a siloed mindset—no matter what the mission statement says. In that kind of environment, leaders will naturally focus on their own targets. Why? Because when performance goals are directly tied to personal compensation or team resources, it's only human nature to prioritize them.

Worse yet, when departmental goals are not just disconnected but in direct conflict, what choice do you have but to compete? When budget allocations happen through a win-lose lens, with just one pot of money and many pairs of hands reaching for it, it creates a zero-sum game. In that scenario, collaboration becomes a risk rather than a strength. And when bonuses are tied solely to siloed success, the system effectively rewards competition over connection. You can't expect cross-functional unity to thrive in an ecosystem that quietly incentivizes division.

True transformation happens when a brand shifts its perspective from thinking vertically to horizontally. This means reimagining how decisions are made, how goals are set, and how incentives are aligned. It requires stepping back, leaning into curiosity, and asking a few fundamental questions:

- What's best for the WHOLE brand?
- What's best for our ENTIRE employee population?
- What's best for ALL of our customers?

> **You can't expect cross-functional unity to thrive in an ecosystem that quietly incentivizes division.**

Let's play with this idea for a moment. We'll say Brand X does this simple exercise, and they decide that what's best for the brand and its customers is to invest in digital. Great. If leaders are operating as a team, they will all be okay watching more money go toward digital, even if it cuts into their budgets. Beyond that, they will approach digital and ask, "How can I help you be more successful...since your success will create success for all of us?"

> **True transformation happens when a brand shifts its perspective from thinking vertically to horizontally.**

Here's my honest take: very few companies actually operate this way. Some *say* they embrace horizontal thinking, but when you look more closely, you often find a traditional vertical structure in place. Departments still work in silos, even while leadership speaks the language of collaboration.

THINKING HORIZONTALLY

I've always tried to organize teams and the way we think as horizontally as possible. I've also tried to protect my teams from verticalization. Thinking and acting horizontally breeds flexibility and inspires curiosity and connections. When it's time to pivot or re-merchandize or shift, a horizontal mindset and structure will help you make the turn.

A horizontal mindset also invites more skin in the game and sets up situations where everybody can and will move faster as a group. It's not about winners and losers. It's about winning together.

Conversely, vertical thinking tends to breed dysfunction. Hierarchies become battlegrounds for power, and leaders get stuck on issues like favoritism, turf protection, and siloed accountability. In that world, people are less likely to ask, "How can I help you succeed?" and more likely to focus on maintaining their place in the pecking order.

Transformation isn't just about strategy but about mindset. And horizontal thinking is where real change begins.

COACHING PEOPLE INTO A *WE* MINDSET

How do you coach others toward building a better, more collaborative system? It begins with clarity—absolute clarity—about what you're solving for. Simply put, you need clarity, because transformation simply cannot happen without a shared understanding of purpose and direction.

That's where your north star comes in. It represents the collective vision of success. In other words, it's your *why*.

Just as crucial as knowing where you're going is being honest about where you're starting from. That takes humility, curiosity, and a willingness to face the truth without flinching.

Simply put, you need clarity, because transformation simply cannot happen without a shared understanding of purpose and direction.

If you're unclear or worse, if you pretend you're further along than you really are, your efforts to evolve will misfire. Not because of a lack of effort but because you're navigating without a true starting point.

Throughout my career, I've made it a priority to align with what the brand was really trying to achieve. Whether the focus was on improving results, boosting profitability, or driving efficiency, I'd start with simple, grounding questions: "What are we trying to move? What's in the way? What needs to change?" And I never answered those alone. I brought them into the room. I invited the team in.

I've always believed the best ideas don't come from individual brilliance but from collective energy, shared insight, and a clear, honest understanding of the challenges in front of us.

When everyone understands the goal, sees the gap, and knows their role in closing it, then momentum starts to build. That's when the conversation shifts from explanation to ownership. And new questions begin to surface:

- How do we do this together?
- What's the first step? What's the next one?
- What's the unexpected idea no one's voiced yet?

This is how transformation takes root and sustains. By helping people see differently, think collectively, and act boldly. That's the power of a *we* mindset in motion.

STAY GROUNDED, BE CURIOUS

Of course, obstacles will come. In any business, large or small, familiar or fast-moving, things will get in the way. Sometimes, the biggest obstacle is the way the organization operates. What can a leader do then? Once again, the answers are pretty simple.

First, stay grounded. Return to clarity. Don't forget the problem you're solving. Staying calm and clear about things can help people stay energized when early momentum wanes. After all, it's one thing to spark excitement but a whole other thing to keep it going—while also nurturing belief.

Secondly, be curious. If you've gotten to this point, then you've probably been curious all along. Don't stop now. Keep asking people questions:

- Do we still believe in the path?
- Is it still worth pursuing?
- Are the setbacks helping us grow stronger?
- Are we getting smarter as we go?

You and I both know that nothing happens overnight. There are always going to be uphill battles. When you stay aligned around belief, clarity of intent, and the steady flow of curiosity, you set the stage for a tireless level of commitment—plus an amazing amount of team cohesion. The message may very well become "Yes, there's some resistance, but here's what we've learned...and here's our next opportunity."

Let me state something very important as it relates to this framework. **Transformation isn't a finish line. It's a return.**

Each time a team achieves real transformation, the journey doesn't end. It resets. But it resets differently: now there's more insight, deeper investment, and a clearer view of what's possible. In its most powerful expression, transformation goes beyond changing outcomes. It widens the aperture of what people believe is achievable.

When belief drives your culture, you don't have to reinvent the destination every time. The north star remains constant. What evolves is how you move toward it together.

You learn. You adapt. You refine. And then you return to the beginning, not as a step back but as a step forward. You reconnect with your people, your purpose, and your belief, this time with more clarity and commitment than before.

> In its most powerful expression, transformation doesn't just change outcomes—it widens the aperture of what people believe is achievable.

That's the real **cycle of transformation**: not a straight line but a deepening spiral that brings you closer each time to who you are and what you stand for. Closer to your north star. And that's where we go next.

A true north star is bigger than any single metric. It's the enduring purpose that guides your brand through calm and chaos.

CHAPTER 10

Moving Toward Your North Star

When you operate from a compliance mindset, you're essentially aiming for the lowest common denominator. I teased this idea back in the introduction. Now as we near the end of the book, I want to shift the lens entirely and start at the opposite end of the spectrum: aiming for your most aspirational, highest-common-denominator destination. That's what your north star is all about.

Do you remember when I asked, "What do you believe?" Here's why I asked: once you gain clarity around what you believe and once you can articulate, illustrate, and codify it, you begin to transform belief into vision and vision into strategy. That's the foundation of your north star, or as I like to call "What you are solving for."

Your north star should be bold, even if it's a little out of reach. Not only is that okay, but it's essential. A little audacity, a little "wow," can go a long way. Your north star should inspire, elevate, and stretch your imagination.

A north star doesn't come with step-by-step instructions that explain how to reach it. It's more about defining a long-term vision, like a guiding light that shows you where to focus and why. The answer to "How will we get there?" will emerge more easily once you are clear on where you are going.

Your north star should be bold, even if it's a little out of reach. Not only is that okay, but it's essential.

When a brand adopts a north star mindset, the process of operationalizing your vision will start to feel remarkably organic. Suddenly, it won't be coming from the top down, but from within.

Your people will begin making recommendations and decisions that align with the vision because they believe in and understand it. That's when you know your north star is truly embedded: when team members see the destination and actively look for ways to get there on their own.

MOVING AHEAD OR SLIPPING BACK?

If your brand knows what it believes and your people believe it too, then why do things sometimes stall or even slide backward? Is it because the organization has become complacent? Started focusing fully on the tactics and lost sight of the vision? Or something else entirely? What gets in the way of north star thinking becoming the norm?

There's no single answer to these questions. Brands slip for all sorts of reasons. Sometimes, people lose pride in the work they're doing. Maybe the energy around them has gone flat. Maybe people are unclear about what the brand is solving for. Maybe the culture has quietly slipped into a status quo mindset, where "good enough" starts to sound like a reasonable goal.

These cultural undercurrents are real and powerful. So let me ask you this: if the brand doesn't genuinely invest in knowing itself and its people, why should those people invest in the brand? And if people don't invest in the brand, why would they invest their time toward helping customers? I'm sure you see the potential ripple effect.

What's the antidote? I'll say it again: clarity of belief. Here's what I mean. Understanding your north star is one thing. Living up to it is another. So, if and when your sense of direction starts to fade, return to belief—not just in words but in actions.

If the brand doesn't genuinely invest in knowing itself and its people, why should those people invest in the brand?

LEADERSHIP CYCLE

Over the years I've spent leading people and teams, I've made it a habit to take complex ideas and distill them into clear, practical frameworks, then provide tools that help others learn, grow, and perform. You've seen several throughout this book. At the risk of one too many, I'd like to share one more that I believe is essential to this conversation.

How leaders think, act, and diagnose problems is critical both for success and for sustained progress. I can't count how many times I've asked someone why a project or result was off track, only to hear, "I don't know… It's just not working." My follow-up was always the same: "What's *it*? What exactly isn't working?" More often than not, they didn't have the clarity or the language they needed to break it down. So I created what I call the **Leadership Cycle**.

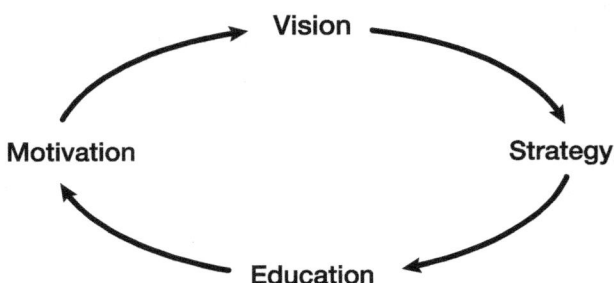

The purpose of this framework is to help leaders think more linearly about action so they can not only move forward with intent but also pinpoint where things break down. Let me walk you through it briefly:

- **Vision** is your north star, which is the destination. Without it, direction is meaningless. But vision has a second act: an honest, objective understanding of where you are today in relation to that destination. The gap between the two? That's what I call *the work*.
- **Strategy** is how you close that gap. It's the roadmap that sequences the work into a coherent plan, whether it takes place over a year, six months, one week, or some other time frame. For that matter, your timeline may change, but the direction stays consistent.

- **Education** ensures the people responsible for executing that strategy have what they need to succeed. That includes tools, training, resources, and clarity.
- **Motivation** is what moves people forward. Sometimes it's positive reinforcement. Sometimes it's an incentive. And yes, sometimes it's a good, well-timed push. But it's always about momentum.

Since it's a cycle, every full turn should bring you closer to the vision while offering insight into what needs to evolve. Its power also lies in diagnosis. When something "isn't working," the Leadership Cycle gives you a way to ask:

- Is the vision unclear?
- Is the strategy flawed or missing critical input?
- Are people lacking tools or resources?
- Are incentives out of sync?

This framework gives leaders a structure to both get clear and stay clear. With clarity, they can move forward with purpose and avoid abandoning progress at the first sign of failure. After all, success isn't about never stumbling. It's about knowing why you stumbled and having the clarity to keep going.

BE INTENTIONAL

When you are clear on what you are solving for, what your north star is, then the decisions you make around delivery, service, and support become clearer and more deliberate. Years ago when I was at Gap, a group of senior leaders gathered in Manhattan, our toughest, most high-pressure market, for a corporate visit. Mickey Drexler, Gap's CEO at the time, was leading us. When

Mickey spoke, people listened. Having him visit and share his vision and wisdom was not an everyday occurrence. When he was with you, he was the focus.

Success isn't about never stumbling. It's about knowing why you stumbled and having the clarity to keep going.

Except for David, our regional manager, whose store we were in. In the middle of the walk-through, David quietly stepped away from the group. He'd spotted a gum wrapper on the floor, picked it up, and then rejoined us like nothing happened.

Later, I asked him about it. "You just broke away from the group...while the CEO was talking...to grab a gum wrapper?"

He smiled. "If I didn't pick it up, what would I be saying? That trash on the floor is okay? That I'm fine with it? I'd be giving my silent seal of approval."

That stuck with me.

His belief in cleanliness and his clarity on how it shaped both employee and customer experience allowed him to make decisions aligned with his north star. When faced with a tradeoff (focus on the CEO or pick up the gum wrapper?) his choice was clear. His intentionality wasn't accidental. It came from knowing exactly what he believed and why it mattered.

MODELING BEHAVIOR

When you're a leader, especially at the highest levels, everything you do is under a microscope. People are always watching. In those moments, your actions speak far louder than any memo or mission statement on the wall. Leadership isn't just about direction. It's about demonstration.

David sent a powerful message that day: no one is too important, and no task is beneath anyone, especially if it means the difference between a clean, cared-for store and a neglected one. Cleanliness was more than just a policy for him. It was a belief, and he acted on it.

This is what it means to model behavior. You can't just tell people what to do. You have to show them. Otherwise, why should they listen to your words when your actions differ?

REMEMBER WHAT GREAT LOOKS LIKE

At the highest levels of leadership, there must be a shared vision of what great looks like and where pride lives in your organization. Everything else should flow from that foundation.

Again, I'm not trying to link things like pride or greatness to money. I'm still focused on intent. Some of this might go against the grain, especially in a world where it's easy to shrug and say, "Well, we just don't have the budget for all of that stuff." Here's the thing: if there's no pride in the outcome or no vision behind the effort, how can you expect people to stay motivated, *especially* if the money isn't there?

> **At the highest levels of leadership, there must be a shared vision of what great looks like and where pride lives in your organization.**

Yes, some things require capital investment. As for pride and intentionality, both are free.

If you're in an environment where employees don't care, take a look behind the scenes. Check the break rooms and back offices. Chances are, you'll start to see why people have lost pride in their work. When there's nothing there for them, that message speaks volumes.

In every brand I've worked with, especially in retail, the mantra around new stores was always the same: dollars per square foot. That single metric dictated profitability.

Back when I started as an assistant buyer at May Co., my desk was literally in the stockroom behind the foundations department. The direction I worked under was simple: if we can't sell it, we don't invest in it. Much more of a head, hands, heart message don't you think?

Now, fast-forward to my time at Gap, during a major reinvention project. Our goal was clear: reignite the brand and the culture and bring back that sense of passionate belief our employees and customers once felt.

As we looked around, something quickly dawned on us: our stores didn't have proper break areas. Employees ate lunch on folding chairs next to shipping boxes, crouched between incoming deliveries.

Before you dismiss this as a small or cosmetic issue, let me say this: it spoke volumes about how we valued our people. We were making zero investment in their environment yet expecting them to invest everything in the customer experience.

Spaces reflect values. If you can't give employees a place to eat lunch, how can you expect them to deliver great customer service? The back of the house drives the front of the house. The internal culture becomes the external brand.

(And yes, we redesigned those stores to include real break areas.)

GO BEYOND MARGINS

Most brand experiences don't involve captive audiences (those audiences that stay with you no matter what). Loyalty is fragile, especially now with options being everywhere. The moment a brand stops aiming high, it starts giving business away. Even brands with built-in demand have to choose how great they really want to be.

Spaces reflect values. The back of the house drives the front of the house. The internal culture becomes the external brand.

Let me illustrate this point further. Picture a hotel chain in a tourist hotspot. Guests are coming no matter what. That chain might think, "We could set the beds on fire, and people would still stay here." They wouldn't, of course, but the thinking is real. Why invest in excellence when people will show up regardless?

Once a brand falls into this mindset—and trust me, plenty do—it becomes obvious they're just trying to do the bare minimum. They're laser-focused on the bottom line, and that's about it. Profit is the only priority. They've stripped things down so much, it's like the brand's soul is missing.

Sure, you might be able to get by with that kind of thinking in a saturated market. For most brands, it's not sustainable. Customer expectations will shift. Market share will move. When you've built a reputation around "being barely good enough," you have very little margin for error.

Imagine you're a customer who had a terrible stay at a hotel on the East Coast. Months later, you're traveling to California for work. You see the same hotel chain. This location happens to be their flagship, the crown jewel of the brand. But that bad memory from the East Coast lingers. Just like that, the California location never gets a chance.

That's what brand continuity means today. One weak link can damage the entire chain. A single poor experience can permanently shift a customer's perception, regardless of how strong the rest of the brand might be.

I saw this firsthand when we introduced NPS to my store team in North America, which I first mentioned in Chapter 6. A lot of that story aligns with working toward a north star.

From the start, we had to redefine what success looks like. In a lot of organizations—and even within ours at the time—success was treated like a zero-sum game. Being top dog was a badge of honor. But for every first-place badge, there's a second place ribbon, a tenth-place pat on the back, a hundredth-place pity party, and so on.

This kind of scoring might make sense internally, but what about for customers? Let's say a couple is used to getting top-shelf treatment in the store downtown. During a trip to the burbs on Saturday, they stop in the same brand's store, except this one is ranked near the bottom of NPS scoring. Bad times ensue. Is this okay? How can a brand be willing to go the distance in one location but completely drop the ball in the other? What does that say about the brand at its core?

We tackled this very issue head-on. To start, we had to reframe around a north star. Our vision was every customer walking out of every store being positively transformed by the experience. NPS was a vehicle for feedback around how well we were doing. Therefore, to succeed we had to have every location delivering at the same level. For a well-run multiunit brand, we decided there should be no more than a two-point difference in NPS between the top-performing and bottom-performing stores.

In my view, this was the right mindset, but it marked a major shift from how things had always been done. It went against the grain of how most organizations approached competition. Many brands clung to the belief that internal competition was healthy and that setting people against each other would drive performance. Create a rival, stoke ambition, and the team will rise to the challenge. That's how the thinking went.

As I see it, when competition turns people into targets or rewards the act of tearing down teammates, then there's nothing healthy about it. We needed to redefine who the real competition was. It wasn't each other. Instead, it was every other brand out there. And the only way to compete externally was to unite internally. If we wanted to lead, we had to work as one. That meant challenging the status quo and reimagining what winning really looked like.

No longer would it be about rewarding the store with the best NPS. Now it was about everyone at every store winning, which was really about the customers winning. It wasn't top-down or bottom-up. It was horizontal in the best way possible. If you were the top store but didn't share your best practices with stores that ranked in the middle, that was a miss. Or, if you were a store in the bottom and didn't reach out to learn from the top, that was also a miss.

Success became a team effort, and its fuel was shared accountability and collective intelligence.

And it worked. Not only did we achieve best-in-class NPS results, but we consistently improved year over year, building on what was already a strong foundation. As for those doubters... they couldn't believe it.

That story speaks to the power of clarity, collaboration, and cohesion. These things can happen when you aim high across the board, not just in spotlight locations. Brands are defined not by their best moments but by how well they meet and exceed expectations again and again, across geography and experiences aligned to your north star.

THE JOB OF YOUR CUSTOMERS

A colleague once asked me, "What role do customers play in helping brands improve? Shouldn't they say something when things go wrong?" My short answer: they don't owe you that. My longer answer: customers have one job, to enjoy a seamless, frictionless experience. Anything beyond that is a gift. The only work a customer should have to do is getting off their couch to come into your place of business or clicking onto your website.

> **Brands are defined not by their best moments but by how well they meet and exceed expectations again and again, across geography and experiences.**

If a customer chooses to give feedback, treat it like the gift it is. Create systems to receive it, acknowledge it, and act on it. This is another place where having your own version of "you said, we heard, we did" becomes essential.

Think about your own experience as a consumer. How often have you left a review, good or bad, and never heard back? Or worse, gotten a dismissive response? When the reply you receive is somewhere on the spectrum between brush off and agitation, trust erodes. It says, "Sorry, but your voice doesn't matter here."

Let's parallel this with your internal customers. If employees feel unheard, they disengage. If customers feel ignored, they leave. Either way, silence or inaction creates distance and breeds disconnection.

Customers are your scorecard. They reflect what's working and what's not, but they won't fix your brand for you. That's not their job. If you're lucky, they might show you where the leaks are before they abandon ship. But the brand needs to fix those leaks on its own.

I want to revisit something I mentioned earlier because I truly can't emphasize it enough: the power of **frictionless experiences**. This is the ultimate prize for consumers in a world where choices are endless and attention spans are fleeting.

The more effort you ask of a customer, the more likely they are to "abandon cart" in every sense of the phrase. People naturally gravitate toward the path of least resistance, unless the payoff is so extraordinary that it's worth the extra work. And let's be honest, those exceptions are rare.

During my time at Apple, we often spoke about how the products were designed to be intuitive. We wanted to remove as many obstacles as we could so users could focus on creativity, content, and experience.

> ## The more effort you ask of a customer, the more likely they are to "abandon cart" in every sense of the phrase.

When I switched my own computer to a Mac, I couldn't imagine going back to a PC. The thought of deciphering the keyboard gymnastics of *alt/shift/command/6* every time I needed to do something felt exhausting. Apple's design philosophy made the technology feel human, as if it anticipated your needs, guided your actions, and just made sense. That's what frictionlessness should feel like. It's not just about being easier. It's about being obvious, elegant, and invisible. This is as true for your employees as it is for your customers.

MAKING IT RIGHT

I want to come back to a mantra I shared earlier: "We may not always get it right, but we will always make it right." I love this statement, but it can only happen if your brand has the mechanisms in place that allow you to actually make it right. What's more, employees also have to have a sense of desire to act on any feedback they receive. It's a reciprocal agreement: you give them responsibility AND authority, and they give you commitment.

Let's say I have a disappointing experience at a restaurant and decide to share my feedback through one of their official channels. Maybe they won't overhaul their operations overnight. Maybe nothing major changes at all. Even just a simple acknowledgment, like a quick email or text, makes a difference. That kind of small gesture says, "You said, we heard." And while the "we did" part may still be in progress, just knowing they listened is meaningful.

Actually, it's more than meaningful. It's a signal of intent. It tells me they care enough to start the process. It's a quiet promise that they're working to make it right and that they're taking the feedback seriously.

We may not always get it right, but we will always make it right.

That sows the seeds of brand trust, but it will only be reaped if the restaurant does something with the feedback. Too often brands overpromise and underdeliver, which creates unnecessary customer dissatisfaction. When silence fills a space, it says, "No one's listening."

That message is toxic. It creates a cycle brands would rather avoid: invite feedback, ignore feedback, repeat. Eventually, people will stop trying. Then they'll stop caring. Then they'll leave.

If you don't respond, you're revealing how you *really* feel about your north star. You're saying, "We're set, thanks. No need for improvement here." That's the absolute enemy of aspiration.

It might even set your brand up as being a liar. Out of one side of your mouth, you're saying, "Hey, look at us, we're employee-focused...we're customer-centric...we want you to tell us about your experience!" Out of the other side of your mouth, you're saying, "Actually, relationships don't matter. We don't care about communication."

The moment you slip into complacency and stop listening to what people are telling you, you've entered lowest-common-denominator territory. At that point, your north star might as well not exist.

Sure, brands don't always have the bandwidth to respond to every piece of feedback they receive. This raises some important considerations:

- If you're not going to respond to or acknowledge people, maybe you shouldn't ask for feedback at all. As I've written, ignoring feedback completely is worse than never asking in the first place.
- Rethink your infrastructure. Build systems that allow you to respond, even at scale. That's how you bring your brand and your vision into alignment with your north star.

Ask, answer, execute. Or more specifically: connect, assess, deliver. Even if that delivery isn't perfect. Which brings me to my next point. The perfection trap.

THE PERFECTION TRAP

In Chapter 8, I wrote about the *satisfaction trap*. Now let's talk about its close cousin: the perfection trap.

The phrase "Don't let perfect be the enemy of good" may be a cliché, but like most clichés, it's rooted in truth. The pursuit of perfection is a trap. It freezes decision-making, delays progress, and creates an illusion that the "right" time or the "perfect" plan is just around the corner. The reality is simple: **perfection doesn't exist**.

When you wait for perfection, you unintentionally stall forward momentum. Instead of advancing, you get stuck in a cycle of tweaking, questioning, and chasing a better version that may never materialize. It's why learning cultures matter so deeply. When teams can test, learn, and adapt, progress becomes possible and even scalable. You give people permission to try, adjust, and improve rather than wait, worry, and stall.

> ## When you wait for perfection, you unintentionally stall forward momentum.

Years ago, I came across Google X—their so-called "moonshot factory," a place where teams were empowered to tackle the world's biggest challenges through experimentation. They were encouraged to try bold, unproven ideas. And crucially, they were allowed to fail. That permission wasn't symbolic. It was structural.

Astro Teller, the head of Google X, once said the following:

You must reward people for failing. If not, they won't take risks or make breakthroughs. If you don't reward failure, people will cling to doomed ideas for fear of the consequences. That wastes time and drains a company's spirit. Finding new transformational ideas is like sending scouts to explore uncharted terrain for new mountains to climb. But if you shame them for coming back empty-handed— no matter how clever or diligent their search—those scouts will quit.

This thinking aligns beautifully with the north star concept. Your north star is the clearest picture of what great could look like. It's aspirational by design, and that's a good thing. I had a boss who used to say, "If you can see it, it can be." Visualizing the ideal state helps people know what they're aiming for. But the real work and value come from the journey, iterations, and the imperfect but intentional steps that move you closer over time.

There is no world in which every decision will be the perfect one. But if you lead with a strong sense of purpose, a compass to guide you, and a culture that allows for trial and error, you stay directionally aligned. You create room for progress over perfection and space for incremental gains that compound into something remarkable.

Your north star should help you break big goals into action-able steps, allowing every decision, investment, and movement to reinforce the larger vision. As I said earlier in this chapter, your north star should be bold enough to stretch you, perhaps even out of reach. But that's not the point. The point is clarity. Because with clarity comes the alignment, focus, and motivation needed to keep moving forward.

At the same time, your vision shouldn't feel so distant that it discourages action. Big dreams should inspire movement, not paralyze it. If the path feels too steep or the destination too abstract, people will lose faith and momentum will fade. The key is to dream ambitiously while building a shared path that others can walk alongside you.

So let me be the first to say: let go of perfection. If perfection is keeping you frozen, you're not in motion. You're not evolving. You're not on the journey. You're stuck. And in the life of a brand, stasis isn't just stillness. It's actually a quiet kind of death.

GOAL OR NORTH STAR?

It's easy to confuse a goal with a north star, and the distinction matters. Say your leadership team proclaims that the north star for the year is to achieve 2 percent growth. That's not a north star. That's a target in the form of a measurable outcome. It's valuable, yes, but not visionary.

A true north star is bigger than any single metric. It's the enduring purpose that guides your brand through calm and chaos. When you mistake a goal for your guiding light, you risk chasing trends instead of building something that lasts. You start reacting instead of leading.

This sends a message to your people and your customers that you're drifting. It says that your brand is more interested in short-term wins than long-term meaning. However, when your brand is anchored in purpose, goals become milestones, not destinations, and tactics serve the vision, not the other way around.

When you say, "We're moving *in this direction* because it aligns with our vision," everything shifts. People understand. The message becomes clear: "We're not abandoning who we are. We're adjusting the path to stay true to where we're going." It also helps to quell the feeling of "flavor of the day," which creates confusion, chaos, and disjointed action.

It might sound subtle, but the distinction matters. It reassures people that your identity is intact and your purpose unwavering. It shows them you're not afraid to evolve. In fact, you're willing to adapt, not because you're chasing some trend but because you're staying faithful to what truly matters. This level of clarity and conviction builds trust, inspires confidence, and keeps everyone moving forward together.

THE NORTH STAR OF RELATIONSHIPS

For a leader, when you're in the business of serving customers and leading teams, there are no off days. The moment you enter that space, you're in it all the way. Remember, relationships are dynamic, either growing or dying. There is no status quo. Things don't stay still. You can't stop investing your own time and energy in the process but expect the relationship to thrive on its own. So the questions all leaders must answer are "What am I solving for in the relationships with my team? What is my north star?"

When a brand stops investing in relationships, it's like they're turning their back on you. Employees will know. They might not turn against you overnight, but it will happen. First, they'll tune out (disengage). Then they'll get angry (disgruntled). Finally they'll leave (disappear).

How can you actually tend relationships, fulfil promises, and move toward your north star? One very simple way is to create and prioritize dynamic touchpoints. Without them, connections fade. With them, trust grows.

Dynamic touchpoints can take many forms, whether regular check-ins, feedback loops, training opportunities, or something else. The format doesn't matter as much. What does is your commitment to doing the work: constantly looking for ways to stay connected and be relevant to employees and your relationships with them.

From the moment a brand hires its first employee, it makes a promise and enters into a relationship. If your brand wants people to invest back into it, then the brand and its leaders have to show them you're invested in them too.

THE JOURNEY AND THE DESTINATION

Your north star may be the destination, but the true magic lies in the journey it inspires. It's not a fixed point on a map but a call to movement. Each step forward becomes part of a deliberate path, guided by a clear sense of purpose. When your destination is well-defined, every decision becomes a choice to align or to stray. It helps you say yes with confidence and no with clarity to what will or won't serve your brand's higher intent.

> **From the moment a brand hires its first employee, it has made a promise and entered into a relationship.**

Progress isn't linear. You will falter. You will misstep. You will refine as you go. But if you anchor your direction to being in service of your people, your customers, and your greater purpose, then even the course corrections become part of the right path. This is what I mean by "making it right." It's not about getting it perfect but staying true to what matters most.

When you believe in the impact your brand can make and

you trust in the reason your organization exists, you begin to see the arc that connects where you've been, where you are, and where you're going. Momentum builds. Progress becomes visible. And every small win along the way is worth celebrating, because each one brings you closer to the future you're working to create.

When belief is alive in an organization—it multiples. It turns culture into movement, employees into ambassadors, and customers into lifelong advocates.

Conclusion

BELIEF IS *THE* ADVANTAGE

Congratulations. You've journeyed through belief not as a feel-good abstraction but as a lived, practiced, sometimes uncomfortable, and always human process. And if there's one truth that carries through every chapter, every framework, every story, it's this: your brand's greatest competitive advantage isn't what you sell but what you believe.

In a world that moves faster than ever before, where algorithms shape trends and attention spans grow shorter by the day, it's tempting to focus leadership energy on what's immediate: quarterly results, market share, operational efficiency. The leaders who will define the next generation of business success do more than manage complexity. They inspire belief.

Your brand's greatest competitive advantage isn't what you sell but what you believe.

Belief is the connective tissue between vision and execution. It bridges purpose and performance. It lives in the spaces between strategy and culture, between what your brand claims and what your people carry forward. And in the noise of competition, belief is the clearest signal of who you are and why it matters.

Throughout this book, we've explored belief not as a soft ideal but as a strategic imperative and a competitive advantage that enables organizations to grow with clarity, to navigate change with resilience, and to cultivate cultures that scale trust, ownership, and innovation.

The leaders who will define the next generation of business success do more than manage complexity. They inspire belief.

The truth is belief drives behavior. When employees believe in the purpose and direction of their work, they go beyond complying. They commit. They bring creativity to problems, care to customers, and courage to challenges. That level of engagement is not a byproduct of strong leadership but the *reward* for it.

Remember, belief doesn't happen by accident. It's something you have to earn, cultivate, and sustain. It begins with clarity and leaders who know what they stand for, why it matters, and how to communicate it without compromise. Clarity builds confidence. And confidence, when shared across teams, builds momentum.

Belief drives behavior. When employees believe in the purpose and direction of their work, they go beyond complying. They commit.

Creating a belief-driven organization means designing with intention, translating purpose into systems, and aligning values with behavior. It's not about posters on break room walls or blurbs in onboarding decks. I'm talking about the daily decisions, actions, and experiences that shape your culture from the inside out.

Your north star—meaning your absolute aspirational vision—matters. And the journey toward it is where belief is built. It will be filled with trial and error, learning and adjusting, listening and leading, and much more that all comes together to create something enduring.

Belief transforms when people put it into practice. And practiced belief becomes culture.

We've covered a lot of ground to this point: ten chapters, three parts, and a framework built to scale belief into action. First, we looked inward at your brand. Have you answered the question "What does your brand believe?" Have you given thought to codifying that belief? Have you made space for employees to align with it, question it, and contribute to it?

Then we looked outward as we moved through the first three phases of the CADET framework: connecting, assessing, and delivering. These aren't optional exercises. They're the foundational practices of any organization serious about building commitment instead of compliance.

Finally, we looked upward and forward into the work of exceeding, transforming, and aligning around your north star.

This final stretch wasn't just about what the brand does but about *who* it is and has the potential to become.

Here's a truth I hope lands deeply: anyone can enforce rules. It doesn't take much to launch a campaign, draft a policy, or issue a directive. But belief is different. You can't impose belief. You can only spark it. Once belief is alive in an organization, it multiplies.

Belief turns culture into movement, employees into ambassadors, and customers into lifelong advocates.

So where do you go from here? Ask the questions that matter most, and be willing to listen in a way that leaves you open to being changed:

- Does what we believe guide and fuel every decision we make for the brand, our people, and our customers?
- Are we investing for long-term success or short-term results?
- Are we building a brand of compliance or commitment?
- Are we managing people or leading them?
- Are we stuck on delivery or daring to exceed? To transform?

The real difference-maker isn't hidden in a strategy deck. It's not a multistep plan or a flashy dashboard of metrics. It's the kind of belief you cultivate with consistency and live out loud. The kind that doesn't just move the needle. It moves people.

CADET isn't a linear roadmap. It's a loop, an ongoing rhythm of listening, learning, building, and becoming. Each phase feeds the next:

- Connecting leads to more human assessment.
- Assessment sharpens the relevance of delivery.
- Delivery earns the trust required to exceed.
- Exceeding earns the right to transform.

- And transformation brings us to a new level of needed connection.

Belief doesn't live in frameworks. It lives in people. It shows up in the store associate who goes the extra mile, in the leader who listens first, in the culture carrier who teaches the "why" behind the work. These are the moments that shape your culture and define your brand.

This is the work of leaders: to serve something greater than themselves and to build the conditions in which others can do the same.

Belief doesn't live in frameworks. It lives in people.

When you invite people into belief...and when they know you trust, empower, and equip them with what they need, they begin to lead with, own, and scale that very same belief into something even greater.

So let go of perfection. Start with conviction. Build the systems. Support the people. Fuel the culture. Strive for commitment. And remember: when you lead with belief, you do more than build a business. You create a legacy.

A legacy built to last.

A legacy built on belief.

Acknowledgments

Writing *Built on Belief* has been a journey of reflection, gratitude, and deep appreciation for the people and experiences that have shaped my path.

First and foremost to my friends—You are the flight and the net, the ones who cheer the loudest when I soar and catch me when I fall. You are my chosen family, my reminder that joy multiplies when shared. You've listened patiently, challenged generously, and believed consistently, even when I couldn't yet see the end of the road. Thank you for the love, the laughs, and the unwavering reminders of what really matters.

To the extraordinary teams I've had the privilege of working with at Apple, Gap, Tory Burch, Bergdorf Goodman, May Co. and Salesforce—Thank you for the countless moments that tested, stretched, and inspired me. You reminded me daily that transformation is messy, culture is everything, and that sometimes the most important leadership tool is a shared laugh behind the scenes. Thank you for showing me what's possible when belief becomes a cultural force. You taught me that excellence isn't an act; it's a habit fueled by purpose.

To the leaders I've worked for—Thank you for your trust, your candor, and the belief you extended to me before I fully believed in myself. I've learned from your strengths, your brilliance, your boldness, and even your blind spots. You helped shape my thinking, sharpen my purpose, and gave me space to share my belief—just as you once shared yours with me. That mutual exchange is at the heart of everything in this book.

To my clients, colleagues, and partners through M2 Collaborative—You continue to inspire me with your courage to lead, your willingness to question, and your commitment to building something better. It's an honor to be your coach, your co-creator, and sometimes your designated "perspective adjuster."

To my students—You've sharpened my thinking and reminded me that the work of brand relationships is never finished. Thank you for challenging assumptions, asking the big questions, and reminding me that belief is not tied to age, title, or tenure.

To Dave Jarecki—I literally couldn't have done this without you and your belief in my voice and my story. Your partnership has been transformational, and your willingness to listen to me prattle on without rolling your eyes is a true gift. Thank you!

And finally to Gunnar and Calla—There is no better example of the power of unconditional love and belief than having a dog. You are both part of my soul.

With heartfelt gratitude,
Matt

About the Author

MATT MARCOTTE is an executive coach, brand strategist, and former senior retail and consumer executive whose thirty-plus-year career spans leadership roles at some of the world's most iconic brands, including Apple, Gap, Tory Burch, Bergdorf Goodman, and Salesforce.

From scaling Apple Retail during its most explosive growth to reimagining customer experience at Gap and shaping employee and customer strategy at Tory Burch and Bergdorf Goodman, Matt has led transformation across luxury, tech, and startup environments. His work is anchored in one belief: people are the engine of every great brand.

As founder of M2 Collaborative, Matt partners with leaders and organizations to unlock human potential through executive coaching, cultural transformation, and consumer experience strategy.

He is known for fusing strategic clarity with emotional intelligence, helping leaders align vision, voice, and values to drive performance with purpose.

Matt is a Columbia University–certified executive coach, an

adjunct professor at Boston College, and a sought-after speaker and guest lecturer.

Built On Belief is the culmination of his career and a call to build cultures of commitment where belief isn't a soft concept but a true competitive edge.

www.ingramcontent.com/pod-product-compliance
Lightning Source LLC
Chambersburg PA
CBHW030511210326
41597CB00013B/867